T0033321

Praise for *Rough*

"A stunning and revelatory memoir."

—*Oprah Daily*

"It's a hell of a story."

—*The New York Times Book Review*

"More provocative than Tur's first book . . . A vivid account of how one woman's inheritance propelled her from a tumultuous childhood to a high-profile perch in television journalism."

—*The Washington Post*

"Heart-wrenching . . . Deeply layered."

—*Daily Mail* (UK)

"If journalism is the 'first rough draft of history' then Tur's memoir is a stunning reminder that journalists are not only providing us with the draft, they are living its revision alongside us."

—*Brooklyn Daily Eagle*

"If you love the kind of true stories that make you say 'omg, how is this real,' look no further."

—*The Skimm*

"Introspective and bitingly funny . . . a thrilling ride."

—*Publishers Weekly* (starred review)

"Raw . . . deeply personal . . . Memoir readers will be captivated by Tur's story."

—Library Journal

"[Tur's] family story is thoroughly involving."

—Booklist

"I don't think I've ever read an account as personal. . . . I really think people are going to love reading this book: for journalism, for life, for families."

—Trevor Noah,
The Daily Show

"Super raw and fascinating. The story Katy Tur tells in Rough Draft is so unusual, but also resonant to anyone with a family."

—Kara Swisher

"She goes all the way there. . . . I see a movie here."

—Gayle King,
host of CBS Mornings

"[Rough Draft] is so good . . . so heroic."

—Nicolle Wallace,
MSNBC host of Deadline: White House

Also by Katy Tur

Unbelievable

ROUGH DRAFT

a memoir

KATY TUR

ONE SIGNAL
PUBLISHERS

ATRIA

New York | London | Toronto | Sydney | New Delhi

**ONE SIGNAL
PUBLISHERS**

ATRIA

An Imprint of Simon & Schuster, Inc.
1230 Avenue of the Americas
New York, NY 10020

Copyright © 2022 by Katy Tur

All rights reserved, including the right to reproduce this book or portions thereof
in any form whatsoever. For information, address Atria Books Subsidiary Rights
Department, 1230 Avenue of the Americas, New York, NY 10020.

First One Signal Publishers/Atria Books Paperback edition May 2023

ONE SIGNAL PUBLISHERS / ATRIA PAPERBACK and colophon are trademarks of
Simon & Schuster, Inc.

For information about special discounts for bulk purchases, please
contact Simon & Schuster Special Sales at 1-866-506-1949 or
business@simonandschuster.com.

The Simon & Schuster Speakers Bureau can bring authors to your live event. For
more information, or to book an event, contact the Simon & Schuster Speakers
Bureau at 1-866-248-3049 or visit our website at www.simonspeakers.com.

Interior design by Kyoko Watanabe

Manufactured in the United States of America

1 3 5 7 9 10 8 6 4 2

Library of Congress Cataloging-in-Publication Data has been applied for.

ISBN 978-1-9821-1818-1
ISBN 978-1-9821-1819-8 (pbk)
ISBN 978-1-9821-1820-4 (ebook)

To my bears, all of them.

CONTENTS

Contents

Foreword

This story is not like anything I've reported for NBC News or MSNBC. It's not a piece of journalism. It's my life and my memories of it, which are a lot like anyone's memories: a mix of old photographs and bedtime stories and dinner table anecdotes and birthday toasts. Plus a lot of stuff that's unique to my parents, like the articles written about them over the years, the interviews they've given, and the contents of a huge digitized tape library, which includes home movies and some oddly modern straight-to-camera monologues, including one surrounded by stuffed bears.

I'm saying all this so you realize that what you're about to read is my best attempt to capture the truth, but also at times the legend. It's the story passed down to me in the form of a legacy. That's also why it matters to me. It's like my parents said, here Katy, here's how we became famous American journalists—can you do the same? As I think you'll agree, no fucking way.

A note about pronouns: if you built a human being from scratch and filled their brain with the *New York Times* op-ed page and the GLAAD media reference guide, they'd never let you down. But I wasn't built from scratch. I had a father, Bob, who is now my father, Zoey. I support her transition and I applaud my father's courage. I also still struggle with my father's past, which is a major part of this book. For that reason, Zoey will be Zoey from the moment of her announcement to me. Before it, Bob will be Bob.

Both she and he will always be my father.

Prologue

This book isn't supposed to exist.

But in the middle of a terrible year in American history, as hundreds of thousands of Americans struggled with illness, and millions of others like me were shut into a kind of forced reflection—the mailman delivered an unusual package from my mother.

Inside was a small, extremely heavy hunk of metal, about the size of an antique Bible: a hard drive containing a digital copy of the thousands of videotapes my mother had been dragging around for years, the output of her and my father's entire careers in journalism. It was my inheritance, of sorts. Every story they shot together, most of them catastrophes. Fires and robberies and car crashes. Their beat was someone else's worst day.

My parents, Bob and Marika Tur, were helicopter journalists in Los Angeles in the eighties and nineties. In fact, they pioneered the form. Madonna flipping off the camera after her clifftop wedding to Sean Penn? That was them. Michael Jackson waving with a burned and bandaged hand in the back of an ambulance? Them again.

They found O. J. Simpson's white Bronco and then carried an

exclusive live feed of the police chase for about twenty minutes, an eternity in TV time, long enough for tens of millions of people to tune in. But perhaps their most consequential footage came out of the Los Angeles Riots. Their images rattled America's second largest city and shocked the country. At one point, their video of the Reginald Denny beating sold for $5,000 per use.

At their peak, when I was in middle school in the early nineties, my parents were on-paper millionaires. They had a seven-figure helicopter (our second), two Porsches (one of them in taxi-cab yellow), a house in the Palisades with a Jacuzzi hut, and enough extra cash to pay private school tuition for both me and my brother. They were famous too, profiled by *People* magazine ("Hot Shots") and *The New Yorker* ("Hot Pursuit"), cheered by the likes of Geraldo and Sally Jessy Raphael. The show *Rescue 911* featured the story of my father finding a transplant patient in the desert.

"Charles Ridgeway, we have your kidney!" he yelled from the helicopter's bullhorn.

In careers as wild as their coverage, my parents were shot at, threatened, arrested, and told off by a long list of people, including cops, firemen, elected officials, celebrities, and their own colleagues. Later, they sued almost every network in the news business, including the one I work for now, accusing them all of unauthorized use of their videos. They won hundreds of thousands of dollars in settlements, but by then the footage had aired and everybody had copied their style, anyway.

Bombastic, propulsive, and live, live, live. My parents shot what is often cited as the first live police pursuit on television, and the second one too—a murder-carjacking that the network decided to air in real time. Instead of a rerun of *Matlock*, viewers watched an actual killer, in a stolen red Cabriolet with the vanity license plate KRUL FA8, run through Los Angeles for forty-five minutes, running lights, jumping curbs. He died in a hail of police gunfire. My parents never cut away.

The next day the ratings showed that the chase was the talk of the city. It had beat *Matlock*, a milestone that helped turn the news into entertainment. Today, some former colleagues blame Bob and Marika for the downfall of local TV news. Some would say the downfall of national TV news too. They don't dispute it. Neither do I.

By the time I was two years old, I knew to yell "Story! Story!" at the squawks of my parents' police scanner. By four, I could hold a microphone and babble my way through a kiddie news report about a fire that ended with a party at McDonald's. By the time I was in high school, though, my parents had lost it all. Their marriage. Their careers. Their reputations. My father in particular was known as one of the most hated people in journalism as well as one of the craziest (which is really saying something).

It's a helluva story.

But I wanted no part of it.

———

Until this very moment, I've been avoiding my childhood and everything about it. When people would ask, I'd keep the focus only on the adventure of it all. While other kids watched *Sesame Street*, I might say, I tagged along with my parents. Instead of being told to cover my eyes, I was free to look down at car accidents, police chases, and shootings.

Sometimes in the middle of the night my parents would rip me out of bed and take me with them to cover an earthquake or a fire. Malibu was always on fire. I'd watch as my mom hung out the helicopter door to shoot video and my dad flew and reported. The heat was so strong I could feel it on my shins five hundred feet in the air.

I might also tell people about the lunches in Catalina just for the heck of it. Or my little-kid driving lessons on my dad's lap, circling the infinite tarmac of the airport. The times my dad turned into the "tickle monster" and made us laugh until we couldn't breathe. I'd tell people about the fun stuff because it was real and we loved each other and that has to be known.

But all these happy memories were haunted too. My father was a charming, larger-than-life figure, a man who scooped the competition on every story and still had time to rescue stranded people in a storm. A man who, when he split with my mom, dated movie stars and tried his hand at feature films. He seemed to keep the world safe and me safe in the world. But he was also a man who punched holes in walls and sometimes tried to do the same to us. A man who, in 2013, called me up and told me he wasn't a man at all.

He was a woman.

"It's why I've been so angry," she said.

That anger was exactly what I'd been trying to forget.

After I published *Unbelievable: My Front-Row Seat to the Craziest Campaign in American History*, I thought the best idea would be to pitch a sequel.

I reminded publishers about the whole backstory. How the editors of *Marie Claire* had asked me to write a personal essay. How they'd watched (along with the rest of America) as then-presidential hopeful Donald Trump insulted me on national TV, called me names on Twitter, and tried to make his campaign impossible to cover. I talked about how I'd turned it all into a first book, which debuted at number two on the *New York Times* Bestseller List (behind another political memoir that year by someone named Hillary Clinton).

Campaign 2020 would be even more *unbelievable*, I said. Donald Trump's presidency was full of feuds and meltdowns, a revolving cast of villains and heroes. I thought I'd keep up with them all, no longer as a correspondent but in my new job as an anchor on MSNBC. "The plan is to take my show on the road, state to state during the primaries, where I'll be in contact with voters, the entire field of candidates, all my old sources, a stable of new ones, and of course President Trump himself," I told the world of book publishing. "The stakes will be higher, the field will be larger, and the gloves will be off."

But of course the gloves stayed on and so did a lot of other personal protective equipment as America spent 2020 locked in, freaked out, and grateful to be alive. Instead of spending 2020 on the campaign trail, I spent it broadcasting from a bunkerlike studio in my basement, alongside my husband, *CBS Mornings* co-anchor Tony Dokoupil.

What I got wasn't so much a sweeping view of American politics as a slightly claustrophobic appreciation of love and my particular marriage. I learned, for example, how to keep a straight face on live TV as my husband burped, farted, and/or napped just feet away from my camera position, often right on the floor in the only kid-free part of our place.

But along the way, I also realized that it's possible for a book that isn't *supposed* to exist to get written anyway—because it *has* to exist. This book, the book you're holding, the one full of stories I never wanted to tell, some not even to my husband, is for me the only possible reaction to a world gone mad. In the past ten years, my father has become a woman, I've become a mother, and our country has nearly become two, split by politics and partisan media, pushed toward outright civil war.

Journalism is known as the first rough draft of history. But at the peak of a lucky career, in the pit of that awful year in America, I found myself thinking through a first rough draft of myself. I hadn't seen my father in years. I was thinking about quitting journalism. I was afraid for the future of the country.

How did that happen? Where did it all go sideways? And what was wrong with me? Was it simple burnout? The aftereffect of the craziest years in modern politics? A by-product of the great, nonstop digital everything? An aftershock of the pandemic? Or was it something deeper, a disillusionment in the value of the work itself?

This book doesn't have it all figured out.

But you could call it a rough draft.

CHAPTER ONE

"I've Decided to Become a Woman"

Always pack a go bag and keep it under your desk.

That's what I was told my first week at NBC News. Not that I needed to hear it. My parents had lived by the same edict. I just ignored it. Or more accurately, I was slow to get around to it. Really slow. Because eight months into my job I didn't have one. And on that day, in April of 2013, I needed one.

I was sitting in the back of a conference room on the third floor of 30 Rockefeller Plaza. The windows faced north toward Radio City Music Hall, the marquee glowing red. It was 2:30 p.m., four hours until *Nightly News*, and the room was packed. Brian Williams walked in and took his seat near the head of the table, next to executive producer Pat Burkey. The other seniors filled out the chairs around a giant conference table. I found a spot on the banquette with the other bleacher people.

Nightly News is thirty minutes long on the clock, but when you subtract the commercials, it's actually just twenty-two minutes of air-time. If you then subtract for daily coverage of politics, international news, and weather, and then subtract some more for a feel-good closing story, you're left with maybe five minutes of airtime for every other general assignment reporter in the building and the bureaus.

That included me.

My strategy was to chime in whenever someone raised an inter-esting idea that wasn't in the rundown.

"Oh that's great," I would say. "We could do it this way or I can go here or there or talk to those people. Or maybe this angle? Maybe that angle? Just put me on TV please."

Desperate as it may sound, more often than not it would work and I would walk out of the meeting with a promise of ninety sec-onds on tape or a minute of live coverage, which, when it wasn't killed—that is, spiked just before airtime to make space for some-thing else—was a good plan.

But on this day, I didn't need to chime in.

I needed to run.

Ten minutes into the meeting, the show's social media producer gasped. He was sitting at the table, laptop open, scrolling through Twitter when he saw the first reports, then the first pictures.

"Whoa," he said. "Explosions at the Boston Marathon."

The room gathered around his laptop. A still photo from behind the finish line showed a big orange and white cloud of fire.

Is that a gas leak?

A steam pipe?

The room went still for a fraction of a second. We were all think-ing the same thing. But you don't go to terrorism right away. You rule out the accidents. There was no video yet. No real information. Still, this was clearly going to be big. Big enough to wipe out the whole rundown. Big enough for me to run.

Brian ran first.

"I'm going to the set," he said.

He moved so fast it was as if he left his voice behind. By the time I looked up, he was gone. Then it was my turn.

"I can go," I said. "I'm going."

I made eye contact with Pat Burkey, but I wasn't waiting for an answer. I was already walking. "I'll call the desk. They'll book me a flight. Delta has a shuttle from La Guardia every hour."

I don't even know if he answered me. Two minutes later I had my purse and I was trying to hail a cab on Sixth Avenue. It was 2:50 p.m. If I got lucky with traffic I could make the 4 p.m. but not if I went home first. *Dammit.* This is why I needed a go bag. I told myself I'd buy a sweatshirt at the airport and wear it under my jacket.

But there wasn't even time for that.

I made the plane, but only just barely and in clothes that weren't warm enough for Boston. But none of it mattered. On the flight, I read the wires and checked the websites of the big papers and followed a steady drip of new details in my inbox. Each ping was another grim fact from NBC's own reporters.

The ride from the airport to Boston Back Bay and the site of the finish line was thirteen minutes without traffic. It would take thirty minutes, if we're lucky, the driver said, and he warned me that there were a lot of closed streets. I checked my watch. Less than an hour to airtime.

"I'll get you as close as I can," he said.

That turned out to be Storrow Drive, the highway that looped around Back Bay, roughly ten blocks from the finish line. It was 6:10 when I stepped out of the car and started my second dead sprint of the day. I took off my heels, striding barefoot over cobblestones, past barricades, leaping off curbs and over planters, waving my press credentials at the cops.

9

I made it to our live location—a couple of blocks from the finish line—with ten minutes to spare. The camera crew had me mic'd up and in focus within seconds. Up to that point, I'd been reading everything I could, but now I needed to streamline it all into a tight two-minute report at the top of the show. I also needed to take in the scene around me.

I talked to a few witnesses, logged the police presence, the National Guard, the roadblocks, the airport ground stop that forced my flight to circle Providence before we could land. I wrote it all down in chicken scratch in my reporter's notebook, and then wrote it all down again, committing what I could to memory. I knew that once I was on television, I had to be in the moment, not in my notebook, not reciting lines but delivering a report.

I also knew that at least ten million people would be watching. They'd be watching because Brian was the best in a disaster but also because nothing beats television when the news is big and ugly and unfolding by the minute.

I took a deep breath and looked into the camera, past the lens and into the inky black behind it. I looked for the pinhole of light, the place where I and everything behind me—the police line, the wounded city—poured in only to pour out the other end as pictures. It reminded me of my parents and it calmed me down. I'd done big, breaking stories before, but not this big. *Nightly News* was the single biggest source of news in America and this was one of the biggest stories of the time.

I heard Brian Williams building to my introduction.

"Let's go now to Katy Tur," he said, "who has made her way up there."

And then I was on.

"We are two blocks from the finish line. Two blocks from where those explosions happened. In fact we saw one woman right over here, witnesses saw her stumbling to this block, with shrapnel wounds," I said trying to slow myself down and project authority. "NBC has confirmed that shrapnel was a part of these explosions. That's why there were so many lower limb injuries. People, witnesses, reported seeing tourniquets being applied on the raceway."

I spoke for more than two minutes, longer than most taped stories that were normally on the broadcast. When I was finished I handed it back to Brian.

"Katy Tur on the streets of Boston tonight," he said, "where for a fifteen block area no one has been allowed."

My heart was pumping. I was exactly where I was supposed to be, doing exactly what I was supposed to be doing. But later when I watched the tape, I could see the live shot was a bit of a mess. I was out of breath. I was talking too fast. I repeated myself. I blanked on a word for a moment. I was in a stupid summer dress on a cold spring day with a scene of absolute mayhem unfolding behind me. Still, I felt a small sense of family triumph. I had run barefoot over blocks of cobblestone and I had made it. I was a Tur.

NBC was the only network with one of their own on the ground. No matter the stumbles, it was a professional accomplishment. A mad dash that secured my place on the most important story of my career to that point and one of the most important of the new century.

I stayed in Boston to continue reporting on the aftermath. The manhunt for the bombers was ongoing. Parts of the city were under lockdown. The attention of the entire country was focused on Boston for weeks. I went home to my hotel each evening, shattered and saddened by all I had covered, but also full of pride. Mom called the first night and complimented my work and we talked about the tragedy. But after a few days, I still hadn't heard from my father.

The last time I had seen him, a few months before this, over the holidays, he was coming back from a week in the Hamptons with a new girlfriend. Not long before that, though, he was in financial trouble, hoping I could help him find a temporary job. He was trying to make a movie, but it was breaking his bank account. He needed me to pay his phone bill.

When he finally called, I was in my hotel room watching local news and eating dinner. It was the first time I'd been able to have something that didn't come wrapped in plastic. My phone rang. I saw his number. I put down my room service cheeseburger, turned down the sound on my TV, and stared at the phone in a moment of choosing.

Do I have the energy for this, right now?

I decided yes. It was my dad after all. Maybe he was just calling to talk about the story.

But no.

That was not at all why he was calling.

In fact, he didn't seem to have any idea where I was or what I had been doing.

"Katy?" he said, his voice going up as he said my name.

It was a tone I knew well. The same tone he had when he launched his run for mayor of Los Angeles. Or his big copyright lawsuit against YouTube. Or his idea to help BP clean all that oil out of the Gulf. It was an octave of hope and desperation in almost equal measure, and I knew even without his saying another word that it meant another change to the way he signed off his emails. He'd tried engineer, chief pilot, environmental scientist, news reporter, dog walker, private detective, know-it-all, and master of the universe.

"Do you have a minute? Are you alone? Are you sitting down?"

Yes, Dad, I thought. *What is it now?*

"Well, I have some big news," my dad said.

I took another bite of my cheeseburger, then nearly choked to death.

"I've decided to become a woman."

CHAPTER TWO

"Like an Angel"

I loved the feeling of liftoff, floating over to the blacktop, nose down, rotors whirling, a bubble of excitement that got stuck in my lungs and made my heart skip a beat. We'd glide to the center of the runway and then it was all speed and light and Los Angeles. Five hundred feet, a thousand, buzzing the beach, waving to the early morning runners and surfers.

On one of the many airborne mornings of my childhood, we put Topanga State Park on our left, the Los Angeles National Forest straight ahead, a million cars not yet backed up on the freeways. In the distance, I could see snowcapped mountains and a big yellow sun. Below me was the city, no center, scattered buildings like blocks on my bedroom carpet, a giant toy set, waiting for me to play.

We headed east for the big party. The parade. My favorite parade. And we found it almost immediately. Then I heard the voice of my father, the voice of my bedtime stories. Except he wasn't talking to me. He was talking to *them*, to everyone below, the people in their cars, in their kitchens, his city of listeners.

"This is Bob Tur reporting . . ."

Through my window I could see what he was narrating, my eyes like a news camera, sweeping over the floats and the dancers. And then a very special float rolled into view, a horse, a gigantic rocking horse, in gold and red with what looked like a stuffed white bear on its back. I wanted a closer look. I wanted to open the doors like I'd seen my mother do, pushing her camera toward the scene. I wanted what she wanted: a clearer picture, a better image.

It was New Year's Day 1988.

I was four and I'd woken up excited for the Rose Parade, a Tur family tradition going back, well, I guess the first four years of my life, after my parents put a baby car seat in the helicopter. How could I not love it? A two-hour parade of color down Colorado Boulevard in Pasadena. Every float was a book come to life. Dancing pandas. A stampede of elephants. A clown doing a headstand.

That year, I wasn't only excited—I was a princess. That's how I felt, at least, because I realized for the first time that my family was different. I wouldn't be watching the parade on television. I would be high above it all. Soaring like Dumbo. The brightest thing in the sky. Because my family had a helicopter. And my father knew how to fly it. And that meant we were special. Which meant *I* was special.

"Like an angel," my father liked to say.

That's what it meant to fly.

My parents were cofounders of Los Angeles News Service, a scrappy little company that covered big, breaking news stories. Their hangar at the Santa Monica airport was the origin point for almost every major television story in Los Angeles between 1985 and 1995, but in between the stories it was also a second home for me and my little brother, Jamie.

Even as a kid, I could tell you which hangar held Harrison Ford's weekend toys. Or Jerry Seinfeld's collection of cars. Or, in a thrill for Jamie and his prepubescent friends, the hangar/photo studio with the naked girls in it. In fact, that one was just next door.

Rock stars and actors flew in and out on private jets, but lots of people hung around all day. There was a restaurant on site, a place called DC3, on the top floor of a building overlooking the runway. O. J. Simpson dined there with his lawyers from time to time. A young Gwyneth Paltrow was on the waitstaff. When I was little, if my parents were on a story, I'd get dumped in the main terminal lobby with a couple of wrinkled dollars for the vending machine. There were comfy chairs and TVs and never mind that every door opened onto a working taxiway.

I was Bob and Marika's kid, the little blond girl who talked like an old pilot. I didn't just ride around on my bike. I was "circling" like my father. I didn't just scarf down mini-boxes of Cheerios and let the crumbs fly away in the wind. I was a junior member of the news team. I knew that if I heard the man on the scanner say, "smoke showing," there was a fire somewhere, and a fire meant a story.

There was always a story.

"We eat out 364 days a year," my father liked to say, "and the other day we're sick."

Inside the hangar, under what had to be twenty-five-foot ceilings, there was a parking spot for my father's Porsche and a two-story office. The bottom floor had a kitchenette, an edit bay, and my parents' ever-growing videotape library. The front half of the second floor had a space for the office manager, aka Grandma Judy, aka my actual grandmother. She was my usual babysitter but she was often busy herself. Just forty-three when I was born, she had a lot of living left to do. My father once found her partying in a Jacuzzi with one of the Van Halen brothers.

She had a phone, a filing cabinet, extra packs of cigarettes, a row of scanners, and a stack of TVs and VCRs. They were partly to monitor the news and partly to track who was using my parents' video. Judy was our enforcer. The person who made sure the family got paid. She was also my best friend in the world. She picked me up from school every day and she'd take me along on all her work errands. We had the same blond hair, same face, same attitude. My nickname was "Little Judy."

In the early days, before my parents were able to electronically feed their footage, Judy's job was to drive the tapes across town to all the news stations in Hollywood and Burbank. I'd go with her, singing along to Rod Stewart as she chain-smoked out the window. Years later, when I got my first job at KTLA, one of my parents' old customers, I'd come across people who still remembered us.

"Man, I loved your grandmother," they'd say. ("Also, how are you a grown-up?")

The back half of the second floor of the office was my dad's workspace, which included a state-governor-sized desk in the center of the room and a wall of accolades directly in front of it. In time, my parents would have so many awards they put some in the bathroom. In that office he was the hero of his own story, a hairy-chested, fearless, fight-you-if-he-must, rescue-you-if-you-need, do-it-all reporter and pilot and family man.

My mother's main hangout was on the other side of the helicopter, on the roof of our "tape library," the final resting place for every day's best stories. In between breaking news, she'd climb to the roof and paint. She had a giant wooden easel, tubes of oil paints, and a style like a California Rothko, all big shapes and bold colors.

She was beautiful herself, working in a tank top, sometimes less. My parents would fly tapes from station to station, dropping them from the helicopter down to the roof where some producer would be waiting. To keep them from breaking on impact my mom wrapped them in anything she had on hand. Usually, that meant her clothing. On a busy news day it wasn't unusual for her to get back to the hangar in only her underwear.

Meanwhile, my dad talked to and entertained an endless stream of visitors. Tours were constant—tours for journalists, for cops and firemen, for machine heads, for news hounds. I'd tag along for those too, thinking my father was the most amazing man in the world and I was his copilot. The one who got to ride along, tinkering with the helicopter, opening this, flipping on that. My father was a perpetual, irrepressible instructor. A certified know-it-all to some, but when I was a kid, an oracle to me.

"The AS-350B or 'Squirrel' is considered a military aircraft," he'd say, walking out from behind his desk and down the stairs to the hangar floor. The big metal bird was always right there, ready to go, sitting on a platform that rolled in and out of the hangar for takeoffs. Once when the Northridge earthquake knocked out power to half the city, my father used a forklift to rip open the electric hangar door and drag out the helicopter. Nothing kept him grounded.

"This baby seats six people, can lift 4,300 pounds, fly 150 miles per hour, has a range of 420 miles, and is certified to go to 16,000 feet. However, it holds a world altitude record of 42,000 feet. That belongs to the French manufacturer," he'd say, with a wink. "Their pilot ran out of fuel or he would have gone higher."

I can still see my father in action, always in a leather bomber jacket and aviator sunglasses, looking like a war hero in pleated dad khakis. One of the many writers who came to profile him once said he called to mind Tom Cruise in *Top Gun*. But he preferred his own living legend to the stuff of Hollywood. He was Chopper Bob. He scooped the competition. He'd say it all the time.

As in: "What does Los Angeles News Service do?"

Answer: "We scoop the competition."

It felt like at any moment the world might split open for some poor soul and my parents would be thrown into action.

Sure enough, on most days, that's exactly what happened.

———

My parents started working as journalists the same night they started dating.

My mother was a graduate student in Philosophy, twenty-three years old, still living at home, working the ticket counter of the Bruin Theatre near UCLA. My father, meanwhile, was at the intersection of self-destruction and fabulous success. He was eighteen, but he told people he was twenty-one. A high school dropout and a runaway, he had somehow secured a GED and a job driving an ambulance. He was already a hand grenade of a man, in other words, but a charmer too, and full of energy.

"I remember him as a blur," my mother said.

He'd visit my mom at the ticket counter, tell her she was beautiful, and ask to take her picture. He'd also ask her out on a date. It took a month before my mother agreed. But what my father had in mind wasn't your typical night out. He'd heard about a school nearby that had been vandalized, so he proposed they take some pictures, try to sell them to the *L.A. Times*.

Side note: It's a little hard to imagine now, but journalism was a hot profession in 1978. Magazines and television companies were fat and rich. The work of their news teams had just ended a presidency and helped close out a war. To borrow a line from an old magazine writer I know, journalism in the seventies was a "get laid" profession. And who doesn't want to get laid?

After my parents took the school pictures, my father had another story idea. Why don't they drive downtown to Skid Row, where someone had been stabbing homeless men to death. If they could spot the guy and snap some pictures, it would make their journalism careers in a single evening. My mom was game. It was exciting. *He* was exciting.

"I needed someone to lead," my mother said. "If there's one thing Bob is good at, it's leading—you're along for the ride. It's hard to get off. You just don't know what's going to happen next."

They went back to skid row on their second date, and their third. For weeks, instead of dinners and movies, my parents did coffees and stakeouts. They never found the killer, but they did find themselves.

Los Angeles News Service was born.

———

By the time I came along in October of 1983, I was born into a business as much as a family. Los Angeles News Service, LANS, was already five years old and a lot like an older sibling, hogging my parents' attention and always getting what she wanted.

My mother was working the night she went into labor. My dad got a call from a fire department source saying there was a story in the parking lot of KABC. I can't tell you what it is, the source said, but you'll definitely want to get there fast. He was right. Turns out, KABC's own 11 p.m. anchor, an institution in L.A., had been shot in a botched robbery just outside of the station. My parents got there so fast they scooped KABC on the story and then sold the tape back to them. A couple of hours later, over Chinese food, the contractions started. I have a picture of my mother from that night. She's in a blue kimono, not a hospital gown, wandering the halls and looking at a clock. It reads 4:30 a.m. Twelve hours later, I was here.

The next day we were all back home, piled into my parents' first apartment in Santa Monica, where my mom set herself up on the couch with all the baby care essentials: diapers, wipes, burp cloths, onesies, police and fire scanners, a telephone.

If she was going to be sitting there all day doing "nothing," as she put it to me years later, she might as well get some work done too. No use merely *sustaining life.*

Years later, when I had my first kid, I realized this was kind of insane. But for them it was necessary. They were so damn young and their business plan was so damn far-fetched. The years before I was born were hard. The idea of a teenager and a grad student launching a competitive news photo business was exactly what it sounds like today: ridiculous. Scooby-Doo stuff. The idea of that same teenager and grad student growing the business from photos to videos to airborne coverage felt like a fable not a plan.

But that's exactly what my parents set out to do.

No one bought it at first. The Los Angeles Police and Fire Departments refused to give my parents press credentials. The small local papers took their photos, but often stiffed them on the payments. To help pay the bills, my mother took a job as copy messenger at the *Los Angeles Times*. She also wrote freelance obituaries at a rate of $35 a death. My father, meanwhile, stuck with LANS, declaring himself chief photographer.

United Press International started paying him $15 a photo and he sold forty the first month alone. When President Jimmy Carter came to visit San Diego in the fall of 1979, UPI assigned my father the story. It almost ruined him. Although he had a fancy camera bag designed to hold a whole assortment of gear, all he really had inside was a single wide-angle lens. Great for close-ups, but terrible for anything from a distance—and there was no way he'd be allowed anywhere near Carter. Sure enough, the press riser was in the back of the auditorium.

But my father's great gift, in addition to chutzpah and hustle, was an unteachable, almost canine instinct. He was a guy who could find a hole in the fence. By acting like he belonged to the location's audio team, he walked directly into a secured area, made an adjustment or two at the podium, then found a position near the front. Jimmy Carter lost the country. But my father got his shot.

To this day, when I feel the urge to push a little harder, go a little faster, risk a little more in pursuit of a story, it's usually not my competition or my colleagues that I have in mind.

It's my father.

Not that I'd endorse all his methods.

———

My father never needed a reason to think bigger, but the UPI work gave him one and, coupled with a big change in the news business, it set his imagination on fire. In 1980, CNN beamed its way into American homes and the phrase "breaking news" began its long, slow journey toward overuse and cliché. Every show in America suddenly felt the need to get better video, sooner, and my father believed he could deliver it.

This was the Stone Age, keep in mind: A video camera wasn't an app on your iPhone. It was a $40,000 piece of equipment. Even if you could afford it, you'd have to learn how to use it. My father had no money or film experience. He was just a guy on his couch, thinking, yeah, I'll buy one of those and I'll figure it out.

He solved his money problem by looking outside of news. He became a private investigator, documenting people in the act of insurance fraud. The conventional tactic was a stakeout. You'd sit out-side a house and you'd wait. If you waited long enough, the thinking went, your mark would do something self-incriminating—like rake the yard or dance in front of the picture window.

My father started with that approach. But he got tired of waiting, bored sitting in his car outside the house of his mark.

To hell with it, he must have thought: *To break into the truth busi-ness, I'll tell a few lies.*

He got out of his car and made a big show of setting up a loaner camera, a Super 8. Then he started filming from the sidewalk. He drew attention and, as he hoped, someone from the house came out to see what was going on. Then came the lie or, if you prefer, the bluff.

"I'm checking for gas leaks," he said, pointing to the camera. "It has a special lens." He mentioned some reports of trouble in the area. It was enough to get him invited onto the guy's property, where he saw his target. A man who told his employer he couldn't walk was up on a ladder pruning trees.

It went on like that for weeks. These early days were so wild my mom wrote it all down in a memoir she never finished. Time and again, my father got the name of a potential fraudster and then out-bullshitted the bullshitter. Once, when his target was in an apart-ment building and his line about gas leaks wouldn't work, he told a parking attendant that he'd seen someone sideswipe a woman's car. Minutes later he had footage of that woman, who also claimed she couldn't walk, easily walking around her car, bending over to carefully check every inch, and then lifting two large bottles of water out of her trunk. She carried one under each arm and climbed the stairs back up to her home. Yet another "gravely injured" man performed the superhuman feat of single-handedly lifting the engine out of his car.

Before long, my dad had his news camera.

The business of LANS started to boom in the early eighties because my father was willing to do something that—even in a big city like Los Angeles—he says wasn't being done, not with film, not at scale. He worked overnights, the graveyard shift. He'd later claim the movie *Nightcrawler* was based on him. The first night out he covered a fire, a train accident, a small plane crash, and a traffic collision. Then he sold it all to the city's local morning shows. They were hooked.

For a moment or two, he had a monopoly. Then two of his former friends—one of them a partner he shot some of his first overnight footage with—started overnight news companies of their own. That tells you something about both the gold rush of the moment and my father's ability to turn friends into enemies.

The future of the business was still unclear. My mom was not yet working for LANS full-time. While she would help out as she could, she also tried out traditional journalism jobs. After the *L.A. Times* gig, she took a desk job at KNBC. It was steady and reliable. Not at all like her boyfriend, Bob, with his midnight runs for a story, his hundred-mile-an-hour habits, no seat belt, as if the First Amendment guaranteed the press eternal life.

The story that turned LANS into a national player, and finally got my mom to commit to it full-time, started with one of those hundred-mile-an-hour sprints. It was 2:30 a.m. in the summer of 1982 and my father heard over the scanner that there had been a helicopter crash in Santa Clarita with children reportedly among the injured. It didn't make sense. Not the time. Not the location which was way out into the wilderness along Castaic Creek. He called my mom at home, woke her out of a dead sleep, and asked her to confirm it with the Fire Department. She did.

Without an address, just a vicinity, he headed for the brightest lights he could see, got as far as he could by car, and then exited the 5. He followed a nearly dry riverbed straight into the woods. The only thing out in this area was a six-hundred-acre ranch used by movie studios. My father headed toward it and right into the barrel of a handgun. In the darkness, he made out the shape of a large man. A security guard.

"Where do you think you're going?" the man said. "This is a closed set."

Journalism can be a dangerous business. People die pursuing it. They don't usually die near movie sets, however, shot to death by a security guard. It's just not worth it. My father didn't think like that. Not at twenty-two. Maybe not ever.

It took my dad a split second to make his decision.

Would the guard really shoot a trespasser? he thought. *Especially one with a press pass and camera?*

My dad bet, no, and kept walking.

The guard didn't shoot.

A few moments later, my father had his camera on a downed Bell helicopter and three bodies covered in yellow sheets. In the morning, he'd find out the big sheet was covering the actor Vic Morrow, star of the *Twilight Zone* movie. The two smaller sheets were child actors, a six-year-old and a seven-year-old, playing characters being rescued by Morrow. The helicopter had fallen on them, killing all three.

It was the first national exclusive for Los Angeles News Service.

It was also the story that convinced my mom LANS might be a better bet than KNBC. It showed her they could sell footage nationally and that the networks paid big money for big exclusives. Before she could quit KNBC, however, she was fired. On her off day, she went with my dad to cover an unusual earthquake in Mammoth, near the ski resort. She was supposed to be back at KNBC the following day but two developments changed her plans. First, she slipped on some black ice and broke her leg. Second, NBC News, her employer's parent company, wanted the video that LANS was gathering. So, she called out on her shift at KNBC, worked through the pain of her injured leg, and conducted interviews including one on camera. The story had gotten big. The network wanted the video immediately, so it chartered a plane to get my parents and their videotape back. My mom's boss at KNBC saw the tape and fired her on the spot. It was a conflict of interest, he said. She couldn't work for two news organizations at once.

After that, LANS added a third employee, soon-to-be grandma Judy. The best damn news team in the business.

I want to say it wasn't about the money for my father, but the money was nice when it finally came. I remember the change, because I remember not having it for so long. One of the things you notice when you're in a helicopter is people's backyards. When I was little, and my parents were mostly broke, I was mesmerized by people's pools and hot tubs, their gardens and fountains, a whole universe hidden from the street.

A lot of those pools were in the moneyed part of the Palisades. The part we moved into when I was in fifth grade. My parents were renters, because every spare dime went into the business. I didn't know any better. To me our new place was amazing. Two stories, high ceilings, my own room, a spiral staircase, and sponge-painted walls. Very on trend in the nineties. There was also a view of the ocean in the distance.

Best of all, the backyard was huge. It had a giant grapefruit tree that my brother and I would climb up to launch grapefruit "wars" against our friends down below. Then there was the hot tub. It wasn't exactly my dream of a pool, but it had its own little wooden hut with sliding doors. I thought it was the coolest, most magical place I'd ever seen.

Instead of our old hand-me-down furniture, my mom took me shopping for new stuff. We went to the design stores on Melrose with her friend Sharon, a Hollywood set decorator. Mom wanted a Santa Fe vibe, so Sharon helped find big oak bookshelves, a big wooden coffee table, and a green and red couch in a Navajo pattern.

We started traveling more too. Big, expensive vacations. To Maui, where we'd sit on the beach for hours making sandcastles, then sleep off sunstroke in a hotel that only had suites. The pool had a swim-up bar where my brother and I would order fries and virgin piña coladas then race each other to the waterslide. On one trip, I climbed up that waterslide, slipped, and broke off my two front teeth, giving my parents and now me lifetime dental bills.

In the winter, we'd go skiing in Mammoth or Snowbird or Steamboat Springs. Two trips a year. Once for Thanksgiving. The other for Christmas.

At the Chateau Whistler, my mom caught me making out with a Canadian boy named Evan (pronounced ev-ahn). I thought he looked like Josh Charles from *Don't Tell Mom the Babysitter's Dead*. When I failed to check in with my parents, my mother came looking for me. She found me and him on a couch in a quiet corner of the hotel lobby. She was holding one of her super-high-powered news walkie-talkies. I was mortified.

"I found her," she radioed to my father.

We stared at each other for a moment before she clicked the talk button again.

"She's fine."

Back home, my dad bought my mom a Porsche, then crashed

it himself, then bought another one. We also had a Land Cruiser, which my parents drove to interviews at a bunch of fancy private schools. My brother and I got in and my parents covered everything. That left us with little to do but grow up and be happy.

And we were.

My childhood smelled like eucalyptus trees, the Pacific Ocean, and jet fuel. It sounded like flipped switches and the click of a Beta tape into a camera. It felt like a sunburn, a scraped knee, and the heaviness of a helicopter headset. And it tasted like a tuna fish sandwich from The Apple Pan, washed down with water in a paper cone cup.

Los Angeles was the backdrop to it all. I think about the city a lot now when I think about my own kids. They'll grow up talking about different roads, in different ways. They'll think it's weird when I say, "*the* 405," when they just say "95." They won't even know what a "freeway" is and may think Shake Shack is better than In-N-Out. *Christ.* They might even try to put cheese on their tacos. They'll never know Los Angeles as a native. In a sense, I worry, that means they'll never really know me.

———

In 1985 my father walked into the sales office of the Hughes Helicopter company. Here was a guy in his twenties asking for a quarter-million-dollar flying machine with maybe 15 percent down, probably less. His plan was to use it for daily newsgathering, something no one had ever done before. Also, he had no pilot's license and his cameraman was a girl. They laughed him out of the office.

He tried Bell Helicopter next, walking in with a thicket of invoices and the same business plan. This time my father got deeper into his pitch. The Los Angeles News Service would dominate the skies. Revolutionize the news. Beat everyone on everything. And he'd come back to buy an even bigger helicopter. This was just the beginning.

The salesman bit.

That May, my parents took possession of a used white Bell Jet Ranger, tail number N2068B.

Later that summer, Madonna and Sean Penn were getting married in the backyard of a spectacular mansion overlooking the ocean. As the sun set, limousines lined up in front of the mansion, while news helicopters stacked up on the ocean side. My father didn't have his license yet, but he hired a pilot and took the lowest angle, just 150 feet off the bluff.

It was a gamble because he'd lose his big aerials, the easiest payday. But if the newlyweds appeared along the shoreline, he'd get the head-on images. They did and my dad got a special message from the bride. Her middle finger.

Back on the ground in Santa Monica, as my brother and I played on the floor of the office, a stranger knocked on the door. It was Phil Ramey, the self-described "King of Paparazzi." He once rented a yellow submarine to get a shot of Princess Diana on an island, but he'd never seen Madonna flip off a helicopter on her wedding day. He wanted to buy the pictures. So did everyone else. By week's end, my parents had made more than $100,000 in licensing fees from the still pictures alone.

Not long after, my father got into a shoving match with Sean Penn at the airport, all of which ended up in the newspaper. My father put Grandma Judy out as the family spokesperson, telling the *Times* that Bob wouldn't press charges.

"I don't think we're going to bother," she's quoted as saying, in between what I imagine are long luxurious drags on her cigarettes. "I just spoke to Bob, and he said he doesn't blame him for being upset because he doesn't like to be videotaped either."

Isn't that magnanimous? I suspect my father hoped you'd feel that way.

He was a self-taught expert at both getting the story and being the story. In their tape archive, there's a lot of Bob playing to the camera. The style is a mix of Instagram (before social media) and reality television (before *Real World*). The newspapers loved him, quoted him in dozens of stories, all in addition to his regular work on radio and television.

He once made seventeen night flights in gale force winds to rescue dozens of people from a flooded hotel.

"News Helicopter Pilot Risks Life To Save 50," read the next morning's AP headline.

"OCEANFRONT AIRLIFT; HELICOPTER NEWSMAN BECOMES RESCUER," added the *Los Angeles Times*.

My father took a reporter from *The Orange County Register* out over the Pacific, then cut the engine.

"Now here's what would happen if the engine died," he said as the helicopter plummeted toward the ocean, before Bob gently restored control. The reporter gushed: "Tur is a superior pilot."

The hotel rescue alone earned my father a big award from the county, an honor he accepted at a gala later that year. He is beaming in the photos. My mom is looking on adoringly. My brother, Jamie, is bashful, pulling at the sleeve of his dress shirt. I'm the big girl, all of four, up in Daddy's arms. I had the picture framed sometime in my twenties and it's still on my wall today.

My dad the hero, the dependable one, the man of the hour.

———

The height of my parents' career came out of two low points in the history of Los Angeles. The first was the Los Angeles Riots, in 1992, set off by the police beating of Rodney King the previous year. I was just a fourth grader with a science project due the day after the verdicts were read. I had a big plastic tub, a pile of sand, and a bucket of water. I was supposed to demonstrate something called "erosion," and I needed my parents to help me put it all together.

But that afternoon, four police officers were acquitted of assault. None were convicted of excessive use of force. My parents flew straight to South Central and the intersection of Florence and Normandie. They'd been getting tips all week. And now it was happening. My mother slid open the helicopter door, checked her harness, and leaned out, dangling herself over the intersection with a forty-pound camera on her shoulder. She captured shots of a burning liquor store, shattered windows, a growing crowd of people.

I was with my mom's parents, Gerry and Connie, who were glued to the television. I stared at the giant walkie-talkie on the kitchen table, our link to the helicopter on nights like this one. My mother set it to the right frequency before running out the door. It was silent and I was stewing. But I remember my grandfather suddenly picked it up and smashed the big black button.

"Set that helicopter down and get my daughter off," he screamed.

I looked at the television in the other room. My mother's pictures were coming in live and I could hear my father's voice, narrating the scene. He said something about "looters." Then I saw the first images of violence. My grandparents started talking in Greek, a language they hadn't taught me.

Then a van stopped in the intersection. The driver was pulled from the cab, and savagely beaten. My father was trying to help. He turned on a siren on the helicopter, hoping it would scatter people. But the crowd continued to grow.

My father dropped the helicopter down to seventy feet, thinking the sound and fury might scare people. Again, it didn't help, and that's about when my mother's camera found Reginald Denny. His red semi-truck had stopped and he was already pulled from the cab when she focused in on the beating that had just begun. It was even more savage than the last. And you may remember how it ended—with a brick to the head.

As Denny lay in the street, my mother held the picture and my father—for the first and only time I can remember—was speechless. He was helpless and overcome. With anger. With disgust. With confusion. Should he land and try to help or continue to document the scene? Could he? Would it be safe? What was his duty? What was his job?

My parents ignored my grandfather's calls over the walkie-talkie. Or maybe they never heard them. The next morning school was canceled and my grandparents took my brother and me to their apartment. That night my parents found bullet holes in the helicopter. Someone had shot up at the fuselage and the only thing that had saved my mother's life was a battery pack under her seat.

After that, they felt marked for violence. It didn't feel safe to have their kids at an address that people could find. I was sheltered from these details, but not from the moment. My parents filmed for a few more days, then flew to New York to appear on NBC's *Today* show. Meanwhile, Judy sold the footage and then sold some more.

I watched Los Angeles burn on my grandparents' ten-inch TV with rabbit ears, a bowl of Grape-Nuts and cream on my lap. I was mad about my science project but old enough to begin to understand that this was something bigger. A first draft of history and my family was in the middle of it. Journalism wasn't just their identity. It was becoming my own.

———

The raw, unedited footage of the riots aired all over the country, helping establish a new expectation in the public mind. No more waiting for the evening news. No more sanitized video. Fate was co-executive producer of every show in the country. It was a "marriage of technology and tragedy," as the *Los Angeles Times* later described it in a long front-page story about my parents' work.

That marriage came of age with the other mega-story in my family's archive: O. J. Simpson's slow-speed chase in the white Bronco. It happened near the end of the school year, and I remember grimacing at my parents' helicopter as it crisscrossed the sky above my middle school. I thought they were spying on me.

In fact, when my parents finally got home that night, I stared daggers at them. By that point, I thought the cockpit Christmas cards with me, my brother, Jamie, and my dog Daisy wearing flight headphones were "boring." I thought getting picked up at sleepaway camp in a helicopter was "so annoying." I hated the way they'd circle my softball games in the helicopter, shouting encouragement over the loudspeaker. There's nothing like, "Katy Tur hit a home run!" or "Katy Tur, where are you?" to make a self-conscious preteen run for cover under the bleachers. It was 1994. I was in sixth grade and so embarrassed by them I couldn't stand it any longer.

My mother laughed at me.

"Katy, not everything is about you. We were over O.J.'s house."

O.J. had been charged with the murder of his ex-wife and her friend, and that afternoon he was—in the words of police—"in the wind." As in, they didn't know where he was. My father, though, had a hunch. Let's go to Nicole Brown Simpson's grave, he told my mother.

When he flew over the cemetery, he didn't see anything, but he heard something over the radio. Right at that moment police had picked up the chase. No location was given, but my father stuck with his hunch and swung out over the 5 near the intersection of Jeffrey Road.

"We've got him!" he shouted. "We're going up live."

At the time, my parents had an exclusive contract with the local CBS station, which took the feed and my father's narration for the next two hours. When CBS network took the coverage a few minutes later, tens of millions of viewers tuned in from around the country. Over the radio, my father heard that every helicopter in L.A. was being told to "find that asshole Tur!"

They did, of course, but only for a day.

No one thought they'd ever really catch him.

He was a legend by then.

———

One day my parents were eating lunch at DC3, their regular spot at the Santa Monica airport, when they noticed O. J. Simpson's defense lawyers wander in without their client. My mother slipped out to get the camera just in case something developed. This was unbelievable luck or just sheer stupidity, chutzpah, and arrogance from O.J.'s lawyers. How could they not know they were dining in the den of the beast?

A few minutes later, a waitress my parents knew came over to the table. She was crying, almost hysterical. O.J. had arrived and he was looking to place an order.

"I cannot serve him," she said. "He's disgusting. I will not do it."

My father paid the bill and met my mother downstairs, now ready for and expecting O.J. to be ejected from the restaurant. And sure enough, he was coming down the stairs. Marika got the shot up and my father came in hot with a question that shocked everyone who could hear it.

"Mr. Simpson," he said. "What did it feel like—slipping that knife into your ex-wife?"

O.J.'s lawyers were livid. This was not a fair question to ask a man considered innocent in the eyes of the law. It was a question that might get a person fired from a network job, sidelined and dismissed as a serious journalist.

But that was my father in 1996.

O.J. smiled and laughed.

The end of the civil trial was one of the last big stories they ever covered.

By 1998 they were out of business.

CHAPTER THREE

"How Dare You. I'm Your Daughter"

I want to say there are a thousand reasons why Los Angeles News Service fell apart, but the truth is there is just one: my dad's anger. I once tried to make a list of the many things my dad threw at my mom in moments of rage. It included keys, plates, batteries, cell phones, two-way radios, and flight helmets. I'm not even counting palms and fists. Once she was wearing sunglasses when he hit her, driving shards of the lens into the soft skin around her eye socket. I walked into the bathroom to find my mother with a rag in her hand covered in blood, her face still oozing. My father was there too, trying to close the gash with a butterfly bandage. That was him: always the hero; also the harm.

I tried to bury this part of my past. I wouldn't talk about it. I wouldn't think about it. I didn't want it to be a part of my story. The day I gave that up was the day I heard a particular tape in my mother's hard drive. It was an unusual day to begin with. Years earlier my parents had given a documentary filmmaker the entirety of their videotape library and the editorial freedom to tell their story as the filmmaker saw it. The whole family sat for interviews, even me. I didn't want to at first, but after years of asking I finally said yes. In January of 2020, the documentary was set to debut at the Sundance Film Festival. A week before that, the filmmaker was in my living room giving me a private screening—not for changes or notes, but to prepare me.

About two thirds of the way into the film, the picture cut to black and at first I couldn't be sure what I was hearing. There was the roar of the helicopter, meaning my parents were hovering some-where, likely on the back end of a story with their microphones still recording. Then there was an ugly sound, like flesh hitting flesh. Then the sound of my mother crying. Then my father's voice, al-most as clear as one of his live reports on the radio.

"I don't know how to communicate with you except through violence," he said.

Maybe it was something about the way he said it—with exas-peration, annoyance, like it hurt him as much as it hurt my mother. But I knew exactly what I was listening to, a sound that as much as anything else was the sound of my childhood. I'm sure they didn't intend to keep a record of the violence, but they did and I'd heard it. I couldn't unhear it. I had to confront it.

I cried into the sleeve of my sweater as the documentary played on. And when it was over, I went upstairs and cried some more. No matter how sunny our lives had seemed on the outside, no matter how many talk shows my parents appeared on, discussing the joys of working with your spouse, our actual lives were often scary. For my mother it was around the clock. At work and at home.

She could never hang out of the helicopter far enough, or focus on the right thing, or move fast enough. God forbid she pressed the record button twice accidentally, meaning she wasn't rolling at all. Dad would lose his mind. He'd fly downward spirals in the helicopter to make her scared and nauseous, then berate her over dinner. They were thrown out of multiple restaurants because he simply couldn't control himself.

The kind of violence on that tape was an open secret in Los Angeles for years. As the technology got better, when my parents were plugged into the helicopter, what they said and did was automatically sent back to one newsroom or another. It was like a hot mic environment—always on, always recording, someone always listening. Did anyone care? Probably a lot of people. But no one called the cops or, to my memory, confronted my father. At one point an anonymous person at KCBS did edit together a grim collection of "Bob Tur's Greatest Hits" and sent it to my house. My father refused to listen to it. But my mother did, at least for a little while. It would be hard for anyone to make it through the whole thing.

It was more than an hour long.

———

My brother and I weren't spared. When we were small, my father used his belt as punishment. He'd catch us, hold us on his lap, and then strike our bare skin over and over again. It was only recently that I learned this is considered child abuse. Growing up it was just how it was. You made him mad. You got the belt.

Along with my goldfish dying and Jamie getting a *Top Gun*–branded plastic jet for Christmas, my childhood memories are spotted with the time spent with my mom plastering over the holes my father punched in the wall. If the damage was beyond repair, we'd hang one of my mother's paintings and pretend it hadn't happened. We had a lot of paintings on the wall.

Sometimes my father would come in and apologize. He'd ask for forgiveness. He'd tell me he loved me. But in the morning the whole cycle would start again. Every day brought the possibility of an explosion. His anger could be triggered by almost anything, but especially if he thought you were being weak or sad when he thought you should be happy.

On one of our fancy vacations to Hawaii, when I was in seventh grade, I was moping around the way preteens do. I had my period. It was new and it made me emotional. I missed my friends. I worried they were doing fun stuff without me. When I was doing my nails on the floor of our hotel room and smudged a finger, I started weeping out of sheer adolescent confusion.

My father lost it.

"Stop crying!" he yelled at the top of his lungs. "You're in *Hawaii*."

I darted for the closest door as he lunged in my direction. It was a small bathroom in the luxury suite he was proud of that weekend. I locked it and shook in terror as he banged and kicked and yelled. If he broke it down, I thought, he'd hurt me. Really hurt me. I don't know how long I stayed in there, but long enough for him to calm down and leave the room. Long enough to feel safe again.

I put up with it for years. The whole family did.

But by my senior year of high school, I'd had enough of my dad's insults and his anger. When he started laying into my mom one day, I just snapped.

"Fuck off," I said. "Get out. We don't want you here. LEAVE!"

He took two or three hard strides in my direction and I couldn't tell you if he spoke or just seethed. The next thing I knew something hit me in the lip, his fist, a short, sharp jab that broke the skin. I remember the taste of blood.

"How dare you," I screamed. "I'm your daughter."

I punched him back, a solid, straight arm blow to the chest, hard enough to rattle my forearm and make my knuckles crack.

"Fuck off," I said. "Now."

My father left. It was quiet then.

I told my mom we should call the cops. It would send him a message. Tell him this wasn't okay. He needed to get help and stick with it. We spent a lot of time gaming it out. But then we also thought of his name. His recognizable fucking name. If it showed up in a police blotter, there'd be news coverage. Bob Tur arrested for punching daughter, abusing wife.

What would that do except make it harder for my parents to work. Harder for them to make a living. Harder to be Bob Tur, the famous helicopter pilot and family man. My mom shot all the footage but my dad was the brand. I hated the idea of hurting him and us. I hated it even more than I hated how he treated us. So we decided to live with it. We had no choice.

———

People always want to know why. They want to understand what made Bob Tur such a hothead and what made his nice, calm, seemingly normal wife, Marika, stay with him for so long. It's a question I've asked her and myself more than a few times. When it comes to my mother, I'm not sure there's a clean answer. But my father's side of the story seems pretty simple: he was beaten himself.

Bob Tur was born in Los Angeles in 1960 after a pretty nineteen-year-old named Judy Offenberg met an already world-weary garment manufacturer named Jack Tur. Jack had already been married and divorced and fathered a child. As the story goes, Judy refused to marry him unless he cut ties with his first kid. He did. And while the marriage that followed may have always been doomed to violence, I think the loss of that connection—the guilt and the grieving on both sides—darkened every waking minute.

Jack was a gambler. At the racetrack, he'd hand his son Bob the rent money and tell him to protect it, to keep it from him. Then he would beat it out of him. The gambling led to losses which led to evictions or sudden abandonments. Sometimes my dad would come back after school to find the family gone. Other times he'd be shaken in the night and told to leave everything behind.

Along with the sudden evictions, my father suffered sudden acts of violence. Nose broken by his father's fist. Hand stabbed with his father's fork. Face slashed by his father's keys. He is missing a piece of his ear because his father sliced it off. In his mid-teens, my dad ran away. Everything he did after that was a continuation of that first attempt to find safety. When there's no going home, no going back, nothing but the future, you find a way to make it, or you fall apart trying.

––––––

The first sign that my father was more than just daring and fun came in 1980, while my parents were still just dating. There was a fire in the Los Angeles National Forest.

Dad thought some fire pictures could help him grow the business. My mom wasn't so sure it was worth the risk. The pictures would be amazing, yes, but their only car was a third-hand British roadster that used to belong to her mother. The clutch was on the brink, one of the hoses was always breaking, and they were missing a gas cap. Just that morning they'd stuffed a cloth into the hole to stop it from leaking.

Surely my dad wasn't crazy enough to cover a fire in a Molotov cocktail on wheels.

No, no, he promised my mom.

They drove to where the Forest Service helicopters were located and a ranger agreed to take them up in exchange for some free photos of the firefighters at work. The shots were terrific. Back on the ground, though, my dad wanted more. Reluctantly, my mom agreed.

They drove a little farther into the forest, finding a spot where the firefighters themselves were staging for the fight. Dad made another deal for photos in exchange for a ride—this time on a truck into the fire. But he still needed more, so he ran deeper into the woods. While he was gone, the fire changed direction and made a ferocious lunge toward the camp. Everyone was evacuating and my dad was nowhere to be found.

Mom started to worry. She was waiting in the car, watching everyone leave. If the guys with the yellow coats and the hoses and the giant trucks were rushing away, why the hell was the Scooby-Doo photo team of LANS still on the mountain? Embers started to hit the windshield and she closed her eyes, certain that her boyfriend was already dead. Certain she was next.

My mom isn't the kind of woman to panic. She did a graduate program in logic, for God's sake, but the only logical reaction here was fear. She was sitting in a thin piece of sheet metal, hugging a cherry bomb of a gas tank, with a ball of fire right in front of her. Instead of making a run for it, she put her head between her knees and waited.

Sometime later Dad appeared out of the smoke like a startled animal, panting, eyes sparkling, adrenaline pumping. When he got in the car the vein in his neck was so big you could read his pulse. He was clearly enthralled by it all.

My mom, on the other hand, was hysterical. He tried to comfort her as they drove out of danger, but she was beyond being comforted. He tried to tell her about the great shots he'd gotten in the woods, but she was beyond caring. She was scared out of her fucking mind.

Then he did what he'd seen done in his own home, what he'd do again over the next twenty-five years in ours, until the marriage was over and the business was broken and their lives were ruined. He hit her. A slap across the face, not a fist, not this time. He claimed it was to calm her down, reset her nerves like a bucket of cold water. He'd claim he'd seen it in the movies. He'd claim it was a bad joke. To this day my mom will say she was angry with him about the slap, but that she also believed his explanation.

He was kidding, she says.

———

I always felt like I knew why my mother stuck around. There was the marriage, of course. My brother and me. The money. The inertia of a shared life. She also had sympathy for what my father had been through as a kid, himself. She felt like she understood him, and to understand is to forgive. All that is true, and yet I had failed to consider my mother's own ambitions.

She was born in Los Angeles in 1955 to a woman who dreamed of a career. Connie (my grandmother) was born to a rich family of Greek immigrants in Florida in 1918. She traveled the world. To Cuba. To Paris. Back to Greece. She floated across the ocean on luxury liners, rumbled through Europe by train. There's a picture of Connie in Egypt as a child on the back of a camel.

She also loved journalism and journalists. Connie kept a metal press ID card for the Paris bureau chief of *Time* magazine in a locked box for decades. We don't know the story behind it, but we think it's a lost love. A life that might have been.

Connie's problem was timing.

She was a woman of the early-to-mid-twentieth century, which means she felt forced down a particular path of marriage and children, though she fought it for years. After her parents lost money in the Depression, she went to the University of Miami to study biology. She found work in the burgeoning field of blood analysis. She loved it so much she intended to stay with it even after she met my grandfather Gerry, a young man from Brooklyn who wanted to be the Greek Frank Sinatra.

It was Connie's career, not Gerry's, that brought them to California. She worked for a blood bank while Gerry used a college degree in engineering to get into the pool business. She continued to put off children past the age of 30, 31, 32, 33. At 34 her luck ran out. She got pregnant with my mom's older brother and lost her job. Bye-bye career. She got fired or quit. Either way, no such thing as having it all in those days.

My mother wanted her life to be different and Connie did too. Maybe that's ultimately why my father's early episodes didn't scare my mother off. She was willing to deal with some turbulence on the way to a dream. She wasn't willing to live another boring life.

———

After the success of the Denny and O.J. stories, my parents signed a lucrative new contract with KCBS and my father poured a lot of the new money into a million-dollar helicopter. It was larger, faster, more powerful, and better equipped for video. The monthly payments were fine if LANS continued to scoop the competition at the same pace. But my father was wobbling in new ways and taking on a lot of outside stress.

He volunteered to testify in the Denny trial and turned my mother's footage over to law enforcement. In open court, he was the first witness to identify one of the attackers, the second witness to identity the other. Afterward, death threats poured in over the phone, people angry about a white man cooperating with police against four black men. Never mind the context.

To protect himself, my father got a concealed carry permit, a chest harness, and a belt holster. He started carrying a gun, a Sig Sauer 9mm, almost everywhere, keeping it close even at home.

"This is a gun. Don't touch it," he explained to my brother and me, ages seven and nine.

At night he'd sleep with it under his pillow.

Down the hall, I felt a free-floating sense of danger. My father was carrying a gun. He must have a good reason. I trained myself to sleep on my back and in line of sight to the door. If I had to sleep on my side I made sure my back was against the wall so no one could sneak up from behind. When I was a little older, if my parents were out late, I'd leave a kitchen knife or a bat next to the bed. There was never a break-in, but we lived with the possibility. The fear never really left.

My father had health issues as well. He nearly dropped dead in front of me on my twelfth birthday at Knott's Berry Farm, an amusement park in Los Angeles. He clutched his chest, slumped on a bench, struggled to breathe. At the hospital, the doctors said he had a near-total blockage in one of his arteries. A stent saved his life and he went home with the usual recommendations of healthy food, more exercise, and less stress.

But my father always seemed to run on a special fuel called animosity. He had conflict with the FAA, the city of Los Angeles, and the California Air National Guard, all of it tied to allegations of reckless flying. The Fire Department once accused him of flying so low over a blaze that he was fanning the flames—literally. He had problems with just about everyone. A fellow reporter went on TV to call him "the most dangerous pilot in the air and on the air."

My father always won in the end, but each round took a toll

beyond time and money. He lost friends and allies. And then every-thing all at once.

In 1997 KCBS started to approach the people who worked with my parents and offered them contracts to switch teams. The com-pany also secretly built a separate KCBS-branded helicopter and embedded an escape clause in my parents' contract. It allowed them to rip up the contract at will and that's what they did.

When I think about what might have been I think about my grand-mother. If anyone could have fixed things it was Judy.

Every news director, even when they hated my dad, loved Judy. She would drive a hard bargain but she was never hard to deal with. She was fun and funny. A little crass and very blunt. She was always smiling. It probably helped that she wore red lipstick and looked great in shorts.

But Judy was gone.

In late 1997, she went to the hospital with a pain in her toe and doctors discovered she had stage 4 cancer, which had spread through her body. I found out how truly bad it was when in a free period before the end of the school day, I called my parents to remind them to come pick me up.

I got the answering machine at the hangar.

"Hi, this is Los Angeles News Service. We can't come to the phone because we've had a death in the family. Judy Tur died today."

I was on a payphone outside of the school library. I stopped breathing, dropped the receiver, and sat on the ground. Did I just hear what I just heard? Did my parents really just announce my grandmother was dead on an *answering machine*? Was it so important to tell their news clients before they told their daughter?

I stood up, hung up the phone, and walked into the library. I wasn't crying. I was in shock. And I had to sit there with it, alone, for another thirty minutes until school got out.

I tried to tell myself that it wasn't happening. That the machine was wrong. I just saw her last night. She was in the hospital and yes she said she was having a hard time breathing. But she looked alive. Not on the verge of death. She was only fifty-seven.

I couldn't imagine life without her. She was my protector. When I was scared or worried, I'd sleep in her bed and she would tickle my arm for hours, until everything melted away. If that didn't work, she had other tricks. Grilled cheese. A root beer float. Once in middle school, I complained to her about a boy who didn't like me back. "Point him out to me," she said with a wink. "I'll beat him up."

I didn't even say goodbye.

I hadn't even wanted to be at the hospital the night before. I was fourteen and I wanted to be at home, on the phone, talking with my friends. I didn't believe she was *that* sick. I simply couldn't face it. She was everything to me and my brother. In some ways, more my mother than my actual mother. And she was holding us together. If she were here, everything would be different. We'd still be a family.

———

After the funeral, my father fell apart too. Some nights he would sit at the foot of my bed crying. He'd never cracked up so completely before. My parents tried to get up and fight on. They hired a lawyer and sued KCBS for breach of contract. While that case progressed, they also tried to stay on top of their other business. People were always using their video and paying for it. But those were Judy's deals. My parents had her files but not her relationships.

Their monthly revenue slid southward. From six figures to five figures to four figures, even less. Difficult decisions loomed. Move into a smaller house? Lose the fancy cars? The private school? The health insurance? The hangar and the helicopter? The math didn't work on all of it. Something had to go.

I remember hearing that the best way to teach a kid about money is to lose a whole lot of it. That's certainly true. I went from oblivious to aware in a matter of weeks. I learned what a bill collector was and to hang up on them. For continuity and probably pride, my parents decided to stay in the house and keep the cars. They also kept us enrolled in private school. But they also cut our health insurance. And they said goodbye to the two biggest expenses in their lives, the two things that had defined them and our family for so long: the hangar and the helicopter.

On March 17, 1998, two months after Judy's death, my parents took the helicopter out for a last flight, late in the afternoon, the sun low, the light golden. As my father flew, he tried to pre-tape some lines, little introductions to the best stories in the LANS archive, something they might be able to package and sell. My mom pointed the camera at my dad and started rolling. But almost immediately it turned into a fight—a blowup about whether she was keeping the shot straight.

"I don't want excuses," my father snapped. "I'm going to tell you this for the last time."

He seemed to mean it as a threat and my mom seemed to take it that way.

"*Don't* hit me," she said. "I can't tell. I'm doing my best."

Back on the tarmac of the Santa Monica airport, they powered down and my mom placed the camera on the rear seat of the helicopter, looking forward, capturing the instrument panel and my parents from behind. They sat still for a while, shoulders slumped, totally silent except for radio chatter and rotor noise. Then the blades slowly stopped spinning.

Suddenly, these two impossibly adventurous, ambitious people, who found every breaking news story in Los Angeles, who flew above fires and shootings and police chases, were two lumps on the couch. They took down their maps of Los Angeles. Turned off their police scanners. It seemed like they had given up on the job, stopped fighting for the next story.

I felt like I'd lost my idols. Instead of thinking about the future, all their energy went into the past. They managed their tape library, licensing footage where they could, suing everyone who failed to pay. I do mean everyone. My parents owned the copyright on the Denny and O.J. tapes, yet lots of organizations aired the footage without paying for it—under the doctrine of fair use. It's supposed to safeguard freedom of expression, but my parents saw it safeguarding the finances of huge media companies. They sued NBC, CBS, Reuters, you name it. I remember fishing through my mother's closet for something appropriate to wear to court.

That became my future. I'd be a lawyer. If not that, a doctor. Definitely not a journalist. The little girl who had loved the feeling of flight and the adventure of a new story was passing on the family business. In my high school yearbook, I wrote that I wanted to become a Supreme Court justice. My parents supported the idea.

"Someone's always going to need a doctor or a lawyer," my father said.

I left for college with nothing to show from my parents' old life. After loading my stuff into the dorm at the University of California, Santa Barbara, though, my father handed me something wrapped in a cloth. I was seventeen and surrounded by kids in flip-flops.

"For protection," he said.

I unwrapped the cloth and saw my grandmother's revolver, a silver .38 snubnose that my father insisted she carry.

"It's not loaded, but an intruder won't know that."

The truly crazy thing is, I took it. I put it in my nightstand. At the time it didn't even seem weird.

CHAPTER FOUR

"You're Bob Tur's Kid"

My father was always hardest to deal with in between the stories, when everything was quiet, and his own thoughts would sneak in. That's why he kept so busy. Now, there were no stories. Without the steady thrill of flying and the challenge of breaking news, he needed even more to quiet his mind. He started taking something to help—a sleep aid, prescription strength.

His body would fight it, though, and he would say he felt overheated. Instead of nodding off, he sometimes got out of bed and walked out of the house. One night when I was back home from college for a visit, he got into his Porsche, his last symbol of success, and started the engine. Then he turned it off and walked back inside.

He came to find me already in bed.

"Katharine," he said, shaking me.

He was smiling.

"The dolphins are sad," he said.

"The what?"

"The dolphins," he said. "They were driving my car. But they cried because all of the fish fell out."

"Dad what are you talking about? Are you high?"

"I opened the door and the fish fell out of the car," he said. "They fell out."

I started to laugh and he did too. I told him to go back to bed.

The next morning I asked him about the dolphins.

"The what?" he said.

"The dolphins. You told me there were dolphins driving your car," I said.

He didn't remember a thing.

I went back to school, but of course he tried to drive again. My brother told me about it. He heard a commotion in my parents' room and rushed in to find a caveman exhibit come to life. Our father was naked and on the move. My mother couldn't hold him back alone. Together, my mother and brother forced him into the upstairs office chair and tried to tie him down with belts.

But he broke free again and headed for the stairs. They tried to grab his hand, tried to drag him back. They yelled. They pushed. By the front door, Jamie wrapped him into a bear hug and tried to pull him to the ground. But my father shook loose and took a swing at Jamie.

Then he was gone. No dolphins this time. Later, my brother saw pictures of him at a gas station—naked selfies in front of the Porsche. He'd apparently set up the tripod and the timer. He even turned them into prints.

———

In 2003, my parents went to a Christmas party in the Hollywood Hills and my father met a doctor named Dale. They started talking, then flirting, and the doctor playfully needled my father about his sexuality. He said he refused to believe that my father wasn't gay. Never one to lose an argument, my dad brought the doctor across the room to meet my mom, his wife, a woman (see!), with whom he had children (see!). This was supposed to prove some sort of case. But that night, my mother was in a playful mood.

"He's married," my mother confirmed. "But is he gay? That's another matter."

Bob had always drawn a lot of interest from women and he seemed to enjoy it. He often said that the best sex of his life was a hot affair with an older woman—his dad's nurse—when he was still in high school. But my mom decided to give Dale an opening.

"Here's his phone number," she said. "I was hoping someone would take him off my hands."

They went out, Dale and my dad, and after a night of dinner and drinks, they went back to Dale's place. My father later said that the moment Dale swept in from behind and kissed his neck, he nearly passed out. He wasn't into what happened next, the "gay sex thing," as he put it, but the feeling of being held lingered. He said he realized for the first time what it must be like to be a woman.

Around the same time, my mother started dating too, though she says it was only after she and my dad eventually did split. At first it was a secret. Her boyfriend was an old pal of my father's, a journalist too. He and my dad once crawled around in the bushes together outside O.J.'s house, looking for a murder weapon. Steve was fun and adventurous but also kind and already familiar with a lot of the family stories. My mother felt safer, but still not safe.

Drugs kept my parents married for longer than they might have been. My mom got ahold of some pot and learned how to bake it into brownies. They would eat and laugh, and eat some more. Sometimes, on a weekend home, I'd eat some too. Why not? I thought. They seemed to be having so much fun and there was so much less tension. We'd all go to the movies—the same theater by UCLA where my parents met.

But even in these years of pot brownies and sleeping pills, my father could still explode with violence. And it was that violence that ultimately broke my parents' marriage. I knew something was more wrong than usual when they showed up at my college graduation separately and didn't sit together. After I got my diploma, I walked offstage and found my mother in the crowd.

"What's going on? Why aren't you sitting with Dad?"

"We're getting a divorce," she said.

And *this* was the day they chose to tell me their marriage was done? My *graduation day*?

"I'm sorry," my mother said. "But I've done my time."

She'd seen me through college and now she was done. To her, it was her own graduation too, her passage into a life without my dad. Whatever it would be, she knew, it would at least be something less volatile. I didn't get more detail than that until more recently. I asked my mother again—why *that day*? Why couldn't she have waited to tell me until, oh, I don't know, *the next day*.

This time she told me the whole story. The night before my graduation, it turned out, she'd come home to my dad sitting at his edit station, working on a documentary called *Why They Run*. They'd gone through their library and tracked down the people they'd taped being chased by the police. It was one of their more successful efforts at professional life without a helicopter. But the edit was tough. Long-form was different than live news.

"How's it going?" she asked my father.

Instead of responding, he turned around and punched her in the chest. No words, just a fist to the sternum. She moved out and began to cut my father out of her life entirely. While I would see her regularly, I wasn't allowed to tell my father where she lived. She told me it had to be that way. She was scared of what he might do. I knew what she meant.

Still, I was angry.

After college, I moved into the space my mother had left.

"You don't have to move in with your father," she told me.

But I felt like I did.

"You abandoned him," I said. "You abandoned us."

I thought she was being selfish. I thought she had stuck me with the job of being my father's caretaker. I was too young to realize she was being brave. I couldn't yet understand that she was protecting herself. It took me years to realize I should have done the same.

———

Three weeks after I graduated, my mother did step in to do me a favor. She called up an old friend at KTLA and found me a temp job. It was my first time working in a newsroom, but I didn't come in with a clean slate. The assignment manager stopped me in the hallway.

"You're Bob Tur's kid," he said.

I was indeed.

"I remember the way he used to scream at your mother on the radio."

He made a face like he'd just seen an atrocity and then walked off.

The news director would tell me more than once, in reference to my parents, "It's a miracle you can walk straight."

To be fair, it wasn't a straight line to journalism. I wanted to be a lawyer or doctor, but things changed once I started college. Right before I left for UC Santa Barbara, the country was attacked. I watched the Twin Towers burn and thought of my high school friends at NYU. I was desperate to hear from them. But I was also desperate to be there. To see what was going on in New York City with my own eyes. To experience it. To share it.

Looking back, this was clearly a flicker of what was to come, but I still needed to fail the midterm for calculus before I realized I'd never be a doctor. I also needed to appreciate that law school meant three additional years of textbooks and classrooms. And I wanted none of it. I figured out what I did want one spring day in my junior year. My college boyfriend and I were driving back to Santa Barbara after a weekend in L.A. visiting my parents, who were still on pot brownies and borrowed time.

We were talking a lot about work, the real world, when we passed a brushfire and a closed road. A highway patrol officer guarded the entrance. A familiar feeling came over me as my eyes followed the line of first responders. I wanted to be as close as possible to that fire. I wanted to see the smoke around me and the flames at my feet. I remembered the sensation of hovering above fires as a child, mesmerized by the smell and the heat. It came back to me in a rush.

"Let's see if we can get in," I said to my boyfriend.

"Why?" he said.

I pulled up to the officer and pulled out a forged press pass. Other than my grandmother's revolver, this was the only piece of my parents' life that I'd taken with me to school. They had official press passes, government-issued documents that allow working journalists to cross police and fire lines for the sake of public reporting. They needed them to work. Or they had, anyway. I did not need a press pass to work. After classes, I was a hostess at a bar and brewery.

But after Judy's death, my father had decided to paste my school portrait over my grandmother's picture, careful to cover every letter of her first name except the "y."

58

"Now you can cross police and fire lines," he said, handing his daughter in effect a fake ID.

"I don't want to cross police and fire lines," I said.

"You might need to."

"Dad, I'm sixteen in this picture."

"Your hair was short, you look older."

"Dad, it says my name is Y Tur."

"So what? No one looks that closely."

"Dad, it's clearly fake."

"Just hold on to it."

I put it in my wallet and forgot about it. One year passed. Two years passed. Then he was right. I did need it.

"Who do you work for?" the officer asked suspiciously.

"Los Angeles News Service," I said, handing over the ID.

He looked down then back at me and then down again.

Fuck, he sees Y Tur.

"Where's your gear?"

Uhhhh.

"My crew is up ahead. They have the cameras."

"All right," he said. "Be careful."

Was that a smirk on the officer's face? Maybe. Probably. To me it was pretty clear he knew I was full of it. But I never felt better. Even my boyfriend noticed.

"I've never seen you more confident than when you were lying to that officer," he told me.

———

I was excited to tell my father about my new career plans. I had already told my mother and she was all for it. But I didn't want to tell Dad over the phone, so I waited for his next visit to Santa Barbara. I saved money from my hostess gig to treat him to lunch.

I wanted him to see that I was growing up. I wanted to say "thank you." And I wanted to hear him say, "That's great, Katharine. I'm proud of you."

He arrived looking like a big shot despite it all: dark jeans, slim black sports coat, crisp white button-down. He'd gotten stylish and he looked great. I remember making a point of calling him Dad in front of the waitress so she didn't think I was his girlfriend. He laughed. Good, I thought, he's in a good mood. My news will make his good day even better.

"Dad," I said. "I have some news."

He perked up. He loved news.

"I've decided to become a journalist," I said.

"A what?"

"A journalist."

"What happened to being a lawyer?"

"That was the plan, yes. But I don't want to go to law school. I'm done with school."

He looked down at his burger and fries and my breath caught in my throat.

"You might as well practice 'do you want fries with that,'" he said, spitting the words out.

I felt like he was trying to shame and embarrass me.

"You always said I could do anything. Now you're telling me there was an asterisk?"

"You're acting like an idiot," he said.

"You're acting like a jerk," I said.

We argued all the way through lunch and back to the front door of my college apartment, which I slammed in his face. We didn't talk for weeks.

He came around, though, and after college while I was living with him we started working on projects together. Now that he wasn't flying, he was shooting his own video. He didn't mind. In fact he loved it. Flying may have been his first passion but camera-work was a close second. He was always buying the newest technology. High definition when it first came out, then RED, the fancy movie quality rig. Tech that cost tens of thousands of dollars. I never quite knew where he got the money for it. The stuff was more expensive than my college tuition. He used it all for his freelance work at a channel called HDNet and deputized me as his camera assistant. We shot Michael Jackson's criminal trial. We also went to Burning Man, Costa Rica, and New York City to shoot travel pieces. He was helping me but at some point I realized he was also helping himself. He was trying to groom me into being his next business partner. A replacement for either my dead grandmother or his absent ex-wife. Two jobs I didn't want.

My father's place was a tiny bungalow in the Palisades, just a few houses down from our first big family home, the one with the southwestern furniture and the Jacuzzi hut. The location alone must have been torture for my father, a constant reminder of what we'd lost. It was for me. I didn't even have a bedroom in this new house. My father had turned the spare room into an edit bay, leaving me the couch or, as was often the case, his bed—because he wasn't coming home at all.

My father would stay out all night at the Abbey, a popular gay club in West Hollywood. Other times he'd disappear to a nudist colony. Or a festival. He loved Burning Man. Some weekends he'd drive up to San Francisco and hang out in the Castro District. He dressed up as Madonna, "bipolar Britney Spears," and—his personal favorite—"a painted tigress wearing little more than a smile."

He would wake me up in the morning and tell me about his

night. I wasn't fazed by any of this behavior because he had always been so . . . out there. When you live with a person whose most consistent trait is their unpredictability, the unpredictability becomes the norm.

For a while, he also dated Princess Leia. Not a look-alike but Carrie Fisher herself. I don't even know how they met, but they were a match. That was for sure. She had a raspy voice, perpetually smudged lipstick, and a huge personality. She was also wildly generous. She once loaned me a pair of diamond earrings. Another time, she let me bring a few friends to a Halloween party at her house. She wasn't even all that upset when one of my friends came as Borat, in full character, and pissed off Val Kilmer in the kitchen (though she did pull me aside and tell me that he needed to drop the act).

The fact that someone like Carrie could be in my father's life made me feel like his life might be back on an upswing. But it didn't last. At home he'd pitch me on his latest moneymaking venture and tell me what I needed to do to make it work. He'd make plans for us every weekend and get sullen when I told him I had other ideas.

And he'd cry.

He'd tell me his life wasn't worth living.

That he was miserable.

That he wanted to kill himself.

Some nights when he wouldn't come home, and wouldn't answer his phone, I'd stay awake in bed and worry he'd gone through with it. At times I felt like I was the only thing keeping him alive. He'd laugh at me for worrying. I started to wonder if this was intentional. Did he want me to think I was the only thing keeping him alive? Was that his way of keeping me here?

In the fall of 2005, I moved out of my father's place and found my own. I thought the distance would help us. But it didn't. Another year went by and I realized that my father had plans I didn't want to be a part of, and he was living through a crisis I couldn't help. I'm not proud of it, but eventually I did the only thing I could think of that would give me a shot at my own life. With very little idea of what lay ahead, only a certainty of what I would leave behind, I got on a plane.

I moved to New York.

———

What can I say here I won't regret? I met Keith Olbermann through the news director at KTLA. He'd also worked there early on, though when we were introduced in early 2006, he was reaching a high point in his career. He anchored *Countdown* at 8 p.m. on MSNBC. I'd been a fan of the show and I liked him. He was smart, sarcastic, witty, and at the time he was doing journalism that I respected. We hit it off, and when I decided to move to New York—a decision so unplanned and desperate that I had nowhere to go—he offered a place to stay.

My life with my father had become the La Brea Tar Pits, a black bubbling swamp that was swallowing me whole. I needed someone to reach in and pull me to safety. Beyond that I wanted a relationship with an adult, someone who had it all figured out. Keith, with all his confidence and authority, became that guy.

I flew into Newark Airport and he picked me up in a black car. Through the back window, as we reached a now familiar clogged loop before the Lincoln Tunnel, I caught my first glimpse of my new city. It was night, the skyline sparkled. I recognized the Empire State Building and nothing else. I was excited to figure it out.

CHAPTER FIVE

"Princess"

In early 2007, after a few months in New York, I was alone at Keith's place overlooking Central Park and eating dinner from an overpriced French place and getting myself mentally prepared for a big job interview the next day at 9 a.m. I had a bunch of well-rehearsed lines about my qualifications.

I could use a Beta cam.

I could work the tripod.

I knew how to white balance.

I knew how to edit in Final Cut Pro.

I knew it all because I grew up in it all.

I was like a farmer's daughter just looking to switch farms.

That was my pitch.

In the next room, I had picked out a black DVF wrap dress with long sleeves and a hemline to my knees. I planned to wear it under a brown tweed blazer I had picked up at a secondhand store. As I pictured myself striding into the interview and getting the job, I bit down hard on a stale baguette and I felt something snap.

My front teeth were already crappy, a pair of old veneers, a fix of a fix (of a fix) from that time I broke them on a waterslide in Hawaii. Had one of them snapped again? I poked my tongue around and, sure enough, found a stump.

I needed to be at the offices of News 12 The Bronx/Brooklyn at nine the next morning, where I was vying for a spot in the News 12 pilot program for new reporters. The news director had seen my tape, aka my reel, a physical VHS recording of twenty-three-year-old me doing news reports that never actually aired anywhere. The tape was all a demo, a mockup, my way to help my hopefully future boss imagine me as a real reporter.

This was a big deal for me as a young journalist: an audition for a job as a do-everything general assignment reporter. The station was New York's smallest and most local. The actual tagline was "as local as local news gets." And while I might have imagined myself starting out with a grander gig, I wasn't ready for one. What I needed was experience. What I needed was this job. This job was my way to the next job and the next job after that. I was ready to put my best face forward.

But I had no front tooth.

I couldn't call News 12 and cancel the interview. I knew enough to know that journalism was about showing up. But I also couldn't show up with a missing tooth. I'd tell them about the waterslide and the baguette, but honestly would you believe that story? I wouldn't. I'd write down "likely drunk" and decline to offer me the job.

That's when I remembered the dentist office on the first floor of the building.

Was it still open?

I ran down to check, hoping that if it was I could talk my way in without an appointment. It was a decent test, I now realize, for an aspiring reporter. Also a wonderful test of whether I'd retained anything from my eighteen years of living with two journalists.

Could I think clearly under pressure?

Could I act quickly?

Could I talk my way into a place I was not meant to be?

Could I solve a problem?

I could and I did.

The dentist glued my baguette-broken front tooth into my head and sent me off with a warning.

"Don't eat," he said. "And try not to talk too much."

I got the gig at News 12.

———

But I wasn't yet on television.

While I had made it through the reporter trial and then got a full-time job, covering Brooklyn, everything I'd done had either been a tryout or a voiceover. My face wouldn't appear on screen until the news director had approved me for air. I wasn't sure what that meant, exactly, but two or three weeks into the job, I was called in to his office for a review of my abilities.

He leaned back behind his big desk, in his big office, and took on an air of casual truth. He spoke.

Your boobs look too big in your TV clothes, he said with a shrug. He might have said breasts or chest or just gestured with a pencil. I don't remember, exactly. But we both nodded in mutual understanding even if I was mortified at the same time.

The news director wasn't done.

He reached for a binder on his desk. Ladies and gentlemen, I shit you not, it was a binder full of women. He pulled out a half dozen glossy pictures of the sort you might see in the front of a salon at the mall.

I wasn't sure where this was going. I thought I was ready for this kind of meeting. It's the TV business. People were going to comment on your appearance. But I didn't expect some sort of headshot hall of fame. The news director sighed and handed me the photos.

"If you want to appear on camera at my station," he said, "you need to cut your hair."

He pointed to the pictures.

"You can choose from any of these styles I've picked out for you."

I looked at the news director. He wasn't unstylish, exactly, not by the standards of the news business. But was he really an authority on women's clothes and hair? Did telling me my boobs were too big and that I needed to cut my hair like he wanted, not strike him as a little presumptuous, not to mention sexist?

I looked down at the photos.

They were, to put it bluntly, blunt. We're talking severe bob cuts. Hard angles. Terrible streaky highlights. Lots of hairspray.

I wish I could say I told him to get bent. I certainly thought it. But I didn't.

As I was leaving, pictures in hand, the news director added one more requirement.

"Your name" he said. "It's taken."

He was talking about Katie Couric, co-anchor of the *Today* show, one of the most famous journalists of the era. I can't be "Katy" because she's "Katie"? Apparently not.

I don't remember the story, but sometime that summer "Katharine Tur," a twenty-three-year-old with her hair shaped into a hard plastic dome, appeared for the first time on television in New York or anywhere.

I'm happy to say the tape is not online.

"Princess."

That was my nickname at News 12. No one said it to my face, but I heard about it from a friend. I guess I had to prefer it to my other nickname, the one that showed up on the label of all my tapes around the office. Everything that said "Tur" had been changed to "Turd." I felt like I was back in middle school, waiting for someone to sign my yearbook, "Dear Zitface."

I wasn't being hazed. I was being punished. I was a new reporter in a new city and I was supposed to agree to every assignment with enthusiasm and humility. Instead I was confident, some would say cocky, and unlike my father, I wasn't willing to get myself killed for a story. Or at least not any of the stories I was covering then.

One night, at 9:55, the assignment editor—the person in charge of sending people out on stories—told me to go to a small house fire in Brooklyn. My shift was up in five minutes and I was packing my bag to leave. Keeping me around for a story was totally fair. That's the business. But as I looked up the address, and the details, I saw that the story was far away and the Fire Department was treating it as a minor fire. There wouldn't be much of a police or media presence. Which meant that since I was a one-man band I'd basically be there alone, late at night, with a bunch of expensive equipment.

To that point, I'd been borderline cavalier when it came to personal safety. I felt like I had to be, lugging around my own stuff, shooting my own standups, editing my own pieces, and going to some of the more dangerous areas in New York, no matter the time. At one point a cop told me not to risk it, as I headed into an apartment building after dark.

"It's not safe," he told me.

"It's my job," I countered.

But this little fire story felt different. Reckless. I decided to pass.

"I don't feel safe," I told the editor.

She laughed.

"This isn't optional," she said.

"Well," I said, "if you want the footage you can go shoot it your-self. See how safe you feel."

———

Princess Turd recovered but not at News 12. I improved and jumped up a rung with a job with WPIX, a storied old New York news channel. The video of a burning yule log you sometimes see around the holidays—a city version of a warm fire in a country home—was a WPIX invention in the sixties.

My job was freelance but consistent: multiple live shots every day, covering breaking news across all five boroughs of the city. The downside was the hours. I had to get up at 1 a.m. to shower and read-in for a 2:30 a.m. call time at the office. The show aired at 5 a.m.

The other downside: I still didn't know what I was doing.

I found this out when the executive producer of the show handed me back a printed copy of the script I'd written for my first story. It was covered in red ink. He started pointing things out.

"No . . . No . . . No . . . Don't do this . . . That's wrong . . . Where did you get this? . . . No . . . That's not usable . . . Please, no . . . Absolutely not." The only thing that wasn't crossed out was my toss back to the anchor in the studio. I had three months to figure out how to write a package or I'd be gone, he said. Fired. Bye-bye. Replaced by someone who can do the work.

I ended up staying for a year and half and falling in love with journalism and my new city.

Yes, the schedule was brutal. I was going to work as people were still stumbling out of bars and the morning papers were still being printed. But it was also an odd kind of privilege to be awake and sober in the hours before dawn, working, witnessing New York as few people do. I was making the city my own just as my parents had done for Los Angeles.

Some days I'd get on the subway and get off in random places and just walk. I would measure my day by how many blocks I'd covered. Thirty or forty was okay. Fifty was good. If I got to a hundred, I'd feel like I'd really accomplished something. Other days, I'd get off work at 10 a.m. and meet a friend who was also on a morning show. We'd find a place willing to serve us margaritas before noon and watch the normals as they streamed into regular jobs, smelling like shampoo and toothpaste. Their lives felt so conventional while ours felt dark and a little dangerous.

I covered shootings, stabbings, robberies, gas explosions, crane collapses, and fires. Local news is all about tragedies. Wrong turns and outrages that need to be feared or fixed. We put a spotlight on slumlords who wouldn't restore hot water even in winter. We did a piece about domestic violence charges, including resources for the abused. We covered school closures in areas already gutted by public service cutbacks.

Local news is easily mocked and often is, but don't let the occasional bad toupee fool you. National news has sweep and an air of grandeur, but local news is much more likely to tell you something that's going to change, if not your country, your morning, your evening, your weekend plans. Will the subways run? Where are the cooling centers during a heat wave? How are the police responding to crime? What's the city doing to keep buildings up to code? It's not always exhilarating but it's essential. I was proud of the work.

Meanwhile, Keith helped me get better as a reporter. He taught me to imagine an audience of one viewer, not many, and certainly not millions. He taught me that every report should deliver heat or light, or some combination of both, a shorthand for coverage that held power to account or said something new. He told me if I don't find it interesting, no one will find it interesting. And he told me to read books out loud to improve my tracking voice. I chose the latest Harry Potter novel, which I'd bought in line behind Salman Rushdie. I could feel myself getting better as a journalist.

But I paid a price for that relationship. When media reporters found out that Keith was living with a twenty-three-year-old, I became, in tabloid-speak, the bimbo. Photographers staked out the apartment. Editors dug up a photo of me at a nightclub in college. Keith's career never suffered, but long after we broke up I was still "Keith Olbermann's girlfriend" to the industry. For years those old articles were the first thing you'd see if you searched for me online. The whole experience was bruising. So much so that I hesitate to bring it up now. I don't want every headline about me to be about him. And I don't want to go back to that headspace where I felt judged and belittled.

For a long time, I thought I could hear other reporters whisper about me. I was sure that everyone assumed I only had my job because of who I was dating. It made me feel like I had to work extra hard to earn people's respect, and maybe I did. And maybe it actually gave me an edge. But in the process of getting tougher, and stronger, of walling myself off, I also got shyer and more suspicious. When people were nice, I'd worry it was some sort of trap. I didn't trust their motives. And absolutely every time I met a new person, I dreaded giving them my name, assuming they'd look me up online and decide I wasn't worth taking seriously.

I never blamed Keith. We split on good terms and we stayed friends. The problem was the world: sexist, misogynistic, and gross. Even after I was assigned to the Trump campaign, and even today, when people want to criticize my journalism, somebody will bring up Keith. It's still the easiest, quickest way to try to diminish me.

———

I might have been at WPIX for years, but after covering the fall of Lehman Brothers in September of 2008, the crash came for me too. The station cut my hours and I was forced to look for other work. Almost nobody was hiring and almost everybody was firing. The one exception seemed to be reporters like me who knew how to shoot, edit, and present stories all by themselves. I hated being a one-man band, but it saved me when I needed to be saved.

In mid 2009, I picked up a six-week road assignment for the Weather Channel, starting in Norman, Oklahoma. I was a junior part of about a fifteen-person team, following a larger group of scientists. The project was called VORTEX2. My prep work involved, among other research, watching the movie *Twister*, which was based on VORTEX1. It made me think I was in for an epic adventure.

I might see a double twister.

I might see a cow fly.

I might see a semi-truck get pulled into the "suck zone."

I might even fall in love with a khaki'd scientist who looks like Bill Paxton.

No such luck.

But at the Weather Channel, I did get my first real taste of life on the road. Every morning, I'd wake up and prepare as the team tried to read the winds. Then we'd zoom off in the direction of a storm. We covered ten thousand miles and ten states in five weeks and I did dozens of hours of live reporting.

It was priceless experience and I'm happy to say my dad was cheering me on. This wasn't a given in the aftermath of my sudden move to New York. We went nearly a year without speaking.

He thought I had abandoned him, had left because I was ashamed of what had happened to him and his career. We patched it up, somehow we always did, and before long I'd be waking to notes of encouragement and advice.

ANOTHER GREAT LIVE REPORT, he wrote one day.

BE CAREFUL, he wrote another time.

Over the phone, I'd tell him about my adventures on the road. The small towns, the little motels. I felt like I was punching my membership card in some sort of club of breaking news journalists. I basked in his interest.

I told him about one overnight, in rural Colorado, when we stayed in what was perhaps America's worst roadside inn. Tripadvisor still has a page up for the doomed establishment with a too generous 1 star rating. The first review reads: "pigsty."

In my room, which I opened with a shove, the carpet had been ripped up to expose the cinder block underneath. The mint on my pillow was, on closer inspection, dried blood. The water in the bathroom faucet gurgled out brown. I went back out to the parking lot where I noticed one of our video editors getting into her car. She was palming a handle of whiskey and lowering the backseat. She yelled "good night" to the rest of us. Another colleague was fishing around in his trunk for what he called his "chastity sack," a sleeping bag for traveling germophobes. As for me, I looked across the road at the "No Vacancy" sign outside the Motel 6 and prayed for a cancellation. I was in luck.

My dad loved these types of stories, and I loved sharing them. I think it reminded him of life in the hangar back in Santa Monica. It reminded me of it also. We both spent a lot of time in those years looking backwards. Shortly after I moved to New York, I had a dream about my grandmother, Judy. It touched a nerve and I woke up bawling. It was the first time I had cried about her in years.

When I told my father about it, he said he had dreams about her sometimes as well.

"I miss her," he told me. "I miss my old life."

I missed it too.

———

The key to being a good live reporter (or, for that matter, these days, a good social media star) is being yourself. Loose. Natural. Unscripted. Interested in the material, not agitated by it. Print reporters are sometimes taught to tell it like they would in a bar. For television reporters, the same adage is true—not to mention dangerous. There's no five-second delay for the censors on a live news report. No editor to save you from yourself.

Near the beginning of our trip, in Norman, Oklahoma, we'd all go to dinner at a place called BJ's Restaurant and Brewhouse. After about five days there, we felt like locals, and just before we left, during a live TV broadcast, one of the anchors asked me what I'd miss the most.

It was a weird thing to ask. I didn't have deep ties to Norman. I had only been there a week. And frankly, the assignment was to be on the road. So the question kind of threw me. I didn't know how to answer it. The only thing I could think of on the fly was food.

"I'm going to miss BJ's," I said.

Panic, danger, abort, abort, abort.

I was standing next to Mike Bettes, the Weather Channel's lead meteorologist on the story, but I was too mortified to look in his direction for help. What I should have done was laugh and explain myself, but I just smiled and said nothing and hoped no one would notice.

Two seconds after the shot was over, a voice in my earpiece: "Did you just say on my show, 'I'm going to miss BJ's'?"

It was the executive producer.

"Yes, I did."

"You meant the restaurant, right?"

"Yes, a thousand percent, yes, oh my God."

"Well, I guess we'll keep an eye on late night and YouTube."

That executive producer is now the president of MSNBC, Rashida Jones.

But here's the twist I hadn't expected.

Back in New York, I got a call from Gus LaLone, manager and executive producer of the Weather Channel. He liked my work. I think he was surprised, frankly. For him, I was kind of a wild card hire. I didn't have deep experience reporting on extreme weather. I wasn't a meteorologist. I wasn't a road warrior (at least not yet). But if journalism requires you to be a quick study and a halfway decent explainer, I learned that I was both.

I also found it easy to get excited about the work. I didn't grow up with weather. There are barely seasons in Los Angeles. So I enjoyed translating science and expert analysis into everyday conversation. And I knew that it mattered. People in the middle of the country live with a gnawing daily threat, a risk that a tornado might take their homes or their lives. VORTEX2 was an effort to prevent that sort of destruction and that singular fact grounded my reporting. Gus noticed that too.

But perhaps most of all, he liked how natural I was on television, screwups and bloopers and all. To him, they made me not only informative and watchable but can't-turn-off-able.

"You've got it," he told me.

Even then, I realized where I'd gotten it from. My father's live reports were always a mix of anecdote and expertise and always filled with "uhhs" and "umms." He was casual and familiar and even goofy. He'd call every police dog "Rin Tin Tin," for example, as if that were a standard generic term for a trained German shepherd. Other times he'd just go blank but talk through. During a massive flood in the agricultural region of Ventura, he couldn't remember the word "lettuce."

"I'm flying over the . . . uh . . . salad fields," he said on live TV. The salad fields?

He wasn't perfect. But he was real. And that's a big reason why he broke through like he did. It's also a big reason I'm where I am today.

A few months later, the Weather Channel sent me to cover the 2010 Vancouver Olympics, and when I got to my workspace I discovered that it was right alongside the biggest prize in television, the *NBC Nightly News*.

Brian Williams walked by and started carrying on with Jim Cantore, a friend from their many days of storm coverage. Almost on reflex, as if remembering something from the way my dad joked around in the hangar in Santa Monica, I jumped in with a joke or two, which laid the foundation for what happened next.

I walked out of an edit bay the next day and turned down a long hallway toward our shared workspace—just as Brian Williams was walking out of the edit bay next door.

"Hello there," he said, as we fell into an awkward walk in the same direction. "What are you working on?"

I told him and he seemed interested, so I decided to go for it.

"Do you want to watch it?" I asked.

I'm sure he did not want to watch it. I'm sure the most famous anchor in the country did not want to sit down at my laptop, wear my greasy headphones, and watch a rough-cut story by a twenty-six-year-old freelancer for a station best known for weather on the eights. But I had asked and one way or another he said yes. Moments later, he sat there in my little workspace, with my taped-up technology, and watched the whole damn thing.

"It's good," he said. "I'd like to use some of it tonight."

I can't remember what I said next, though it was probably some version of the Beatlemania scream. I couldn't wait to tell my father.

———

By the winter of 2010, we were in a pretty good stretch by our standards. He'd send me notes about the *Sex and the City* movie ("they're aging so poorly") or a sale at Jimmy Choo ("there will be a line"). He also raved about how glorious it was to run the Bay to Breakers, in San Francisco. He jogged it nude and posed with Christian protesters.

"I'll have to blur it," he said, "but you've got to see me."

He was sentimental and sweet too. When I was a kid, my parents had a collection of stuffed bears. They loved these things for reasons that would stump Freud. But that's why my brother and I have "Bear" as a middle name. We were joining "the bear family." One of the first was "Blacky Bear." My father got unofficial custody of him after the divorce and he'd send me pictures of the bear, posed like a tourist on his travels. I loved it.

But another side of my father remained. He often made me feel worthless. It was like he was carrying a bucket of water and his bucket had a leak and the only way he could keep his bucket full was by taking from mine. And so he took. And he took. And he took.

He seemed to think I was being lazy by trying a more traditional route up the ranks of television.

"Come up with something new," he'd tell me. "Find the next big angle," he'd say. "Lead, don't follow."

He didn't seem to understand that we were different people in a different era. I didn't have a helicopter to impress people. I also didn't have a penis to ward off the wrong impression with sources. Had my father ever shown up to a meeting that his subject thought was a date? Was he ever assigned a story on pole dancing as exercise? Did an editor ever ask him, "Do you have stripper shoes you can wear?"

"I'm not you," I told him. "I'm doing it my way."

Meanwhile, he was still trying to figure out his own way forward. Although more than a decade had passed since he lost the helicopter, he hadn't found a steady new outlet for his work. Certainly nothing with the pay or recognition of what he did before. The older I got, the more I understood how hard it must have been for him. He was on top of the world at thirty-eight but unsure of his place by fifty.

I was sympathetic. I wanted to help and I did. I gave him a little money, some contacts, free labor for Los Angeles News Service. I cheered him on as he pitched his big idea for a national helicopter service, Newscopters.net. "Welcome to the future of broadcasting, cable, G3, and mobile news technology," his promo began.

In 2006, he became the first person to sue YouTube for copyright infringement, accusing the company of publishing hours of LANS footage without permission. I followed the case as it turned heads and generated coverage for years. In 2007, *GQ* called him a "maverick" in a long profile. My dad ultimately dropped out of the case. But for an instant billionaire and HDNet owner Mark Cuban was reportedly considering an "8-figure" offer for LANS.

Dad also started appearing on television more, mostly Fox News, doing analysis for *Hannity & Colmes* or *The O'Reilly Factor*. He was great on anything related to aviation, or law enforcement, or first responders. He seemed to need more fame and recognition, though, and to secretly believe the rest of us demanded it too.

If I acted like a twentysomething with a life of her own, he was liable to take it as a brush-off. He was paranoid and accusatory, always a victim, the whole world against him, even his own daughter.

"What have I done to deserve the cold shoulder?"

"Is this what you really want? To sever all ties with your father?"

We went long stretches not talking or just yelling past one another. He'd blast off notes across three different email addresses.

Subject line: "FROM DAD."

Greeting: "Katy Bear."

Inside there were guilty reminders of the good times, our family trips, shared books, the way we watched *X-Files* every Sunday. Then the heavy emotional artillery. My dead grandmother would be "devastated" at my behavior. My uncle was embarrassed by how I had treated him. All I cared about was money and the fact that he didn't have much was the real reason we weren't closer. In one email, he listed off all of his professional accomplishments, his whole résumé, in detail.

"TWO Edward R. Murrow Awards."

"TWO AP National Breaking News Awards."

"FOUR Golden Mics."

"SEVERAL heroism awards."

In closing, he referred to his own YouTube lawsuit as "trailblazing."

Like a town slowly rebuilding after a disaster, though, we'd reopen the relationship. After months of not talking, we'd see each other over the holidays. Chat about cute dogs and good movies. Act like father and daughter again. That's what I wanted. I loved him. I still do.

Two years after impressing Brian Williams at the Olympics, I got a chance to do a story for *Nightly News*. I was still working at WNBC, the NBC-owned and -operated station in New York, which had offered me a job after the Olympics. The national network invited me to pitch story ideas a few months before my contract was up.

At the time, NYC was finally building the long-awaited Second Avenue Subway line and a producer and I got to go underground to see the work. I wore a hard hat and toured the construction. I talked to the engineers and watched in awe as a giant machine twisted its way through Manhattan bedrock. The piece was like a visit to Fraggle Rock. My dad called afterward to say, "nice job."

"Your hair was a mess," he added. "Bring a comb next time."

Thanks, Dad.

Like I've always said, the best hair advice comes from balding older men.

He laughed and I did too.

As long as I never brought up the real ugliness of the past, the violence and the abuse, and as long as I ignored the unwanted criticism, we'd be fine. We weren't always easy in each other's company, but we were stable.

———

The end of 2012 and first few months of 2013 were some of the most exciting of my career. I was young and on the rise, starting to break through at *Nightly* by sheer force of will. The key was the morning and afternoon meetings. I learned the only way up was to prioritize being there, live and in person, and ready to raise your hand with a smart comment or a simple "I'll take that on."

For me, the meetings had the depth and reach that I craved coming up through local news. Cutbacks across the industry meant that as a general assignment reporter in local, you barely had time to think. I was out the door seconds after I walked through it, live on multiple stories a shift, often within minutes of getting to the location. Most of the stories were crime. The newscasts were dictated by the latest squawk of the police and fire scanners. There'd be a break in the shopping cart attack. Or the taxi turf war. Or the Pelham Park pedophile. My last story at WNBC was about a handyman who was breaking into a woman's apartment and violating her puppy. That is not a euphemism. It's what the police say was happening to the dog.

"Are they trying to ruin you?" Brian asked, genuinely confused about why my managing editor would waste time in the newscast on a random gross weirdo.

To be fair, after it aired, the station realized its mistake and wiped the video of the report from the internet.

This is all a long way of me saying, the *Nightly* editorial meetings were my salvation and I always showed up feeling fantastic and ready to talk my way into the lineup.

On April 15, 2013, a pair of pressure cooker bombs exploded at the Boston Marathon, and I rushed out to cover it.

I wasn't prepared for what I'd find.

CHAPTER SIX

"Bob Tur Is Dead"

I'd had one bite of my cheeseburger, sitting cross-legged in the middle of the bed. The plate rested on the sheets in front of me while I reclined on the pillows behind me. I was exhausted and starving, drained by four days of round-the-clock coverage of the Boston Marathon bombing. Now my first meal not out of a wrapper in days was over before it started.

"Katharine?" my father said.

My dad was talking on speaker, but I wasn't really listening. Not yet.

My eyes were still fixed to the television screen. There was a breaking news update. An officer shot at MIT. Could this be part of the manhunt for the second marathon bomber? Maybe I should get dressed, I thought. Go back to the stakeout position.

I picked up my phone to text my producer.

"Katharine!" Dad said, louder this time.

"Hi. Sorry. Hi. Yes, I'm here."

"I asked if you're alone."

"Yes. I'm sorry."

I regretted picking up the phone. I wanted to focus on what was happening in Boston. I wanted to get dressed and figure out where I should go. Or I wanted to rest. I didn't want to have what I assumed would be another conversation with my father about a big plan and how I needed to be a part of it. I didn't understand what he was talking about—until he said it again.

"I've decided to become a woman."

I paused this time, giving him my full attention.

And I do mean "him." Because in this moment, in these first re-velatory seconds, that's still how I thought of my father. In telling this story, and looking back, I don't want to pretend I flipped a switch in my mind, erased thirty years of habit, and shifted effortlessly into she/her. I supported my father immediately, but it took a conscious effort to get the words right, and I want to be honest in the telling.

"A what?" I said.

"A woman."

I paused again.

"Are you serious?"

"Serious as a heart attack."

"Dad, *what*?"

He, now she, told me she had felt wrong forever and that she was finally confronting it. She told me she had been born with a "feminized brain" and a male body. She told me this "wrong body" was the root of everything or at least everything wrong in our lives. She had been in denial about her true self.

"It's why I've been so angry," she said.

She sounded almost giddy.

"It's amazing how much better I feel."

I started asking questions.

"Have you told Mom? Have you told Jamie?"

She had. They were supportive, she said. Jamie at least.

"Your mother is confused but deep down she knew," she said.

I was the last person she needed to tell.

"Can we all talk before you go through with it? Have a family meeting?"

Intellectually I knew that this was her decision, and hers alone, but emotionally I felt a desire to take this leap together as a family. Subconsciously I think I also wanted an excuse to get all four of us back in the same room. Part of me also wondered whether she'd actually go through with it. Maybe becoming a woman would be this year's version of Newscopters.net, an exciting idea that we all talk about but somehow fails to come together.

"No," she said. "I already started taking the hormones."

My heart started to beat faster. My breath caught in my throat. The television screen slid out of focus as I realized that this wasn't a discussion or an idea. It was an announcement. I felt lost.

"What do I call you?" I wondered.

I started to cry.

"Are you still Dad? I can't call you Mom."

She laughed and I wondered if maybe she was enjoying this, reveling in my confusion and tears. Did it confirm for her that I still cared? That she still mattered? That she could still affect me?

"Do you still want me to be Dad?" she said.

"Of course, I do," I cried. "No one else is my dad. You are my dad. Words don't change that. You can't just change that. Nothing can change that."

"Then I'm still Dad."

85

The mood lightened. We began to joke and laugh, a little, talking about the shift in pronouns. I started to feel new parts of my own brain rewiring in an attempt to get them right. The hardest part was marrying the phrase "my father" with "she," as in, "My father, she likes makeup." But in fact, she does like makeup. We talked a lot about the clothes *she* would get to wear, the makeup *she* should try.

My father, *she*, went into Sephora and got a tutorial, she told me, and she loved it. I tried to picture my dad in there, trying on lip gloss, testing concealers, experimenting with liquid eyeliner. This was months before *Orange Is the New Black*, before Laverne Cox became a household name and then the first trans person on the cover of *Time* magazine. Two years before Caitlyn Jenner would introduce herself on the cover of *Vanity Fair*. Being trans wasn't yet part of a mainstream national debate, a conversation about rights and respect and acceptance. I felt unprepared and clumsy. I wanted to know more. To really understand. But the conversation, like virtually every conversation we had had over the last ten years, was a roller coaster in the dark. I never knew whether I was headed for a drop.

"You can do a story on my transition," my father said, changing the subject. "The *Today* show should have us on together."

I didn't know what to say.

"No, really," she continued. "Embrace it. It's the new thing to do and you're right on the leading edge."

My father's career had been all about being "on the leading edge," one step ahead, seeing where things were going before anyone else. This was no exception.

"Oh, Katharine," she said, a foretaste of fame already in her voice, "this is going to be great for your career."

Maybe so, but I didn't see this as a way to get ahead or get publicity. I also knew that if I said "no" outright my father would snap at me. The conversation would become a fight. I also sensed that my father wasn't really floating a notion about media exposure. She probably already had a plan in mind to pitch her transition as a documentary or a reality TV show—to own the story and be the story.

"We'll see," I said.

"Don't be stupid," she snapped.

I told her we'd discuss it later. I needed some time to process. I told her I was proud of her and that I loved her.

"No matter what," I said. "I love you."

———————

She told me her new name was Hannah. It meant "grace" in Hebrew. This part was less surprising. My dad had always had spurts of wanting to be more Jewish. She'd occasionally take us to temple or buy a menorah and make latkes on Hanukkah. For my dad it was more cultural than religious. She liked the tribe, wanted to be a part of it. She also openly wished she'd married a Jewish woman. A Jewish wife would have expected more from her and pushed her to be a success, Dad would say. She wouldn't have let her fail. Not like my mom.

We talked on.

"I'm already a worse driver," my father said.

Wait, what?

"I started to take the hormones and they're already changing the chemical makeup of my brain. It's amazing, Katy. My brain is shrinking down to the size of a woman's."

I scoffed.

"It's true, a woman's brain is smaller. It's biology."

"And that's what is making you a bad driver?"

"Yes. It's science. I can't make decisions as quickly as I used to."

"Dad, what the fuck. Women aren't genetically bad drivers."

"Katharine, don't be mad. It's biology."

I started to get annoyed. Here was my dad telling me about life as a woman because she'd read an endocrinology textbook. She also rattled off jokes so retrograde they'd get you booed out of a retirement home.

Now that I'm a woman, I look forward to always being right!

I'm a bad driver, but suddenly so good at asking for directions!

Sorry, but I now talk during movies and roll my eyes when men talk about sports.

But what really got us lost was my father's detour back into the past.

"Katy Bear," she said, with an air of self-exoneration. "Don't you see. *This* is why I've been so angry my whole life."

If my dad hadn't brought up the anger again, we might still be speaking. I might have continued to hide from it, and our relationship, however dysfunctional, might still stand on that foundation. Denial can be powerful. But my father wanted more than denial. She wanted the memories thrown out, the records expunged, and that idea forced me into a confrontation—with my father, with our past.

"We need to talk about the violence," I said.

She refused.

"But we need to do it," I said. "I need to do it."

She refused again.

It felt like my dad was playing a get-out-of-gender-free card I didn't know existed.

"I already feel different," she said. "My female brain is getting softer and more emotional. I'm filled with calm and love. I've changed."

I was dumbfounded by the idea that a person could change their gender—align it, confirm it, become their true self—and think that in the process the deeds of the past would no longer be relevant. It was ridiculous to me, like a bank robber pleading not guilty on account of gender misalignment.

But that's how my father saw it.

"Bob Tur is dead," she finally told me.

The words struck with an almost physical weight.

"The stuff Bob Tur did isn't dead," I tried to explain. "You yelled. You hit. You caused pain."

She denied it.

"Who did I hit?"

"All of us," I said. "You even kicked the dog."

She denied it even harder.

———

After the call, I pulled the sheets over my head. I wanted to go to sleep but my mind was racing. I turned the volume back up on the TV, hoping it would drown out my thoughts, and eventually I fell asleep. At some point in the middle of the night I woke and my mind returned to the implications of my father's announcement.

I tried to think of what she must be going through. My dad was always so out there sexually. I thought of the nudist colony, the cross-dressing weekends, the gay bars. But also the bullhorn of straight white maleness. My dad flew a helicopter. My dad drove a hundred miles an hour down the highway. My dad wasn't afraid to throw a punch. My dad wore leather bomber jackets and baggy khakis. Until recently my dad's favorite pair of shoes were sneakers that looked like a Ninja Turtle. Total dad wear. Liked them so much she bought them in multiples.

And yet.

I thought back to a conversation we had about a longtime sports columnist—another straight white male—who had come out as transgender. She wrote a column about it. My dad sent it to me and asked me what I thought. We talked about it a lot and I decided she was being brave. Maybe my father had been testing the waters.

I also remembered a joke my dad made last month. It was a dumb little comment attached to an email from something called "Millionaire Dates." Probably spam but I don't know for sure. It was a personal ad from a man. It read: "Looking for an attractive, smart and ambitious woman to keep me company and allow me to spend my riches on her."

My dad forwarded it to me.

"Do you think I should go out with him?"

"Sure," I wrote back. "Why not?"

"Do I look like a fracken woman to you?" my dad replied. "Not yet anyway."

Maybe I'd been blind. Maybe this really was an explanation for everything.

"I hope you can support me in this," Dad had said at one point in our conversation.

"Of course, I can," I promised.

But what were her needs? What were my own? How could we move on from this point in a way that might be healthy for both of us? I knew I needed space to figure it out.

———

We met at a Mexican restaurant in Mar Vista and sat outside.

The first thing I noticed about my father was that her hair was getting longer. Goodbye, pattern baldness, I thought. She was excited about it too, and already planned to dye her hair blue as soon as she could. We laughed at the idea and in her smile I could see that the hormone therapy was definitely working. Her facial hair was thinner, her features softer, her clothes clingier. She wasn't yet wearing anything of the sort you'd find in the woman's section of a shop. One of her rules was to wait on women's clothes until the transition was complete.

I'd been trying to prepare myself for these changes and more. The last time I'd seen my father, six months earlier, she'd still been Bob Tur on the outside. Now she'd started to change, shifting names again from Hannah to Zoey, which she said meant "life." Zoey was still my father, still familiar—but in other ways a stranger at the same time.

One of the only bits of continuity from past to present was my father's dog. Leica is a cairn terrier, a rescue that had brought out a new side to my father. Dad had her registered as a service dog so she could bring her everywhere. I thought back to when I was a kid. Our family dog was a poodle named Daisy who had perhaps the family's biggest battles with the old Bob. She'd walk into my dad's room, look at him, and pee on the carpet without breaking eye contact. If we were play-wrestling with my father, Daisy would join in to bite him. It didn't matter if we were pretending to attack my dad or my dad was pretending to attack us. He was the one who got bit.

I know why she hated him. He was mean to us and he was mean to her. He had a habit of throwing our toys out the window of the car. Anything we bickered about got the toss. One day we fought over the dog and he threatened to throw her too. We believed him. We'd seen him be rough with her. At the end of her life, he made her sleep outside to save the carpet she'd been peeing on. She got eaten by a coyote out there. But as with us he could be sweet with her too. They'd nuzzle and snuggle. When she died he threatened to kill the coyote.

The new dog and I shared what felt like a meaningful glance as my father and I settled into a conversation. Leica growled when I reached for a menu in the center of the table. She didn't care for me. In fact, she didn't like anyone without a penis. Women made her defensive and aggressive. I wondered, in all seriousness, whether Leica would keep loving my father after the transition.

"She'll remember the smell," she assured me.

We ordered chips and salsa and I decided to say what I'd come to say.

It'd been a long two months since my father's call, and a wild twenty-four hours since she'd taken the news public, joining TMZ for her first interview as Zoey just the day before. Not the outlet I would have chosen, but then again I wouldn't have chosen any outlet at all. TMZ founder Harvey Levin and my father were old friends from local news in Los Angeles.

I was in town for work, had just landed, in fact, when the appearance aired. I watched it later, through splayed fingers in my hotel room. My father appeared via webcam, wearing a black button-down. Over her shoulder I saw Blacky Bear on a shelf by the microwave.

It wasn't so bad. She recited some questionable science, claiming, as she had with me, that the hormones were changing her brain, and hurting her talents as a pilot. She also talked about her timing, the way she'd withdrawn from society, cut off friends, sunk into depression, before realizing that the only cure was to live as herself. She also confirmed that she was indeed considering a reality TV show.

Then she talked about me, acknowledging that I was going through "a mourning process," that we all were. It made me think that my father and I were seeing the same problem, searching for the same solution. I arrived at dinner hopeful that we could fix it together.

And so I tried.

"I know this is what you want," I began, trying my hardest to strike a calm tone. "I know this is what you need to be whole. I will support you. Always. I'm on your team. You're my dad. I think what you're doing is brave."

I wanted this to sink in.

"I also understand that Bob Tur is dead to you."

She smiled. A good sign.

"You, however, are still alive and sitting across from me and are my father. That's the person I have a history with and I'd like to talk it through with *that* person."

The smile disappeared and we sat in silence.

"Can we do that? As you reset your life, can we also reset for me, and Jamie, and Mom, and the people who have been in this life with you for all these years?"

My father dragged a tortilla chip back and forth over a scoop of guacamole.

"Dad, seriously, I understand that you don't want to do this. But you did a lot of crappy things when we were growing up."

No response.

My father wanted to throw the past into the abyss and let it sink while I needed to dig it up and lay it out for discussion. There was simply no getting past this difference, though we both tried.

"I've changed," she said. "I've changed. I've changed. I'm a new person. This is a new me. All that is gone. I've fixed it."

She spoke with exasperation.

"It's all over," she said. "I'm happier and I'm nicer. I don't have any of those emotions any longer."

She placed her palms on the table and leaned forward toward me. The disconnect between the words and her face was stark. The words said, reasonable request from a sane person. The face said, you don't want to keep messing with me. It was a face I knew well.

I tried but I don't think I could have really imagined how this must have felt for her. How she'd done the hardest part. How she'd come out and risked it all. Wasn't that enough? What more could I want? I took her hands in mine, clasped them in the center of the table, and tried to show her how much I cared about making this right between us.

"Let's get through it," I said.

She yanked her hands away and looked me directly in the eyes.

"You're a selfish, disgusting person. You only care about yourself. Your boyfriends. Your career. You never ask about me. Never ask how I'm doing. What I'm doing. If I'm okay. You are a terrible person," she said.

I could feel people looking at us in the restaurant.

"I never want to see you again," she told me.

And then she got up and left.

A moment later the waiter came over, looking confused.

I thought about ordering a margarita. A shot of tequila. But it was L.A. and I had to drive back to my hotel.

I took the check.

CHAPTER SEVEN

"Send Me Now!"

I wanted to run and six months later, in early 2014, I got my chance.

The call came in to my boss, the New York bureau chief, who sat behind me in an open office in 30 Rock.

"Uh-huh . . . Yup . . . Uh-huh . . . Got it . . . Sounds good," he said.

He hung up and swiveled around in his chair.

"Hey Katy, they want you to go to London for a couple weeks," he said. "Bureau duty."

The phrase was magic to me, a dream. It may sound like "jury duty" but this was not the kind of assignment people try to avoid. The job was to work on a temporary basis in the London bureau of NBC News and be ready for anything. Have you seen *Broadcast News*? It was a compliment to be asked, a vote of confidence and a potential investment in me. Overseas experience is traditionally a prerequisite for the bigger jobs in the industry. And although the offer was only for a ten-day change of scenery, it felt like a chance for a ten-year refresh on my soul. I clapped my hands and said yes.

Three days later, I got off a plane in Venice, Italy, and almost immediately boarded a water taxi. That's just how it's done in Venice. You brush off the airplane crumbs and step onto a polished wooden yacht that looks like it's on loan from George Clooney. The air smelled sweet and clean and the sun sparkled off the canals. My career to that point had consisted of the five boroughs of New York and familiar old America. Now I was rushing through a city that felt like a rumor, pursuing my first overseas assignment: a Venetian vote over whether to break away from the mainland, to secede from Italy, and go it alone.

But in a bigger sense, of course, I was the one breaking away, seceding from my life in America. In the months after my father told me she never wanted to see me again, I'd thrown myself into work rather than risk a moment of introspection or insight. Journalism is the world's best career for avoiding your own problems. After a while, though, I needed something new, something stronger to keep me from replaying the dinner, second-guessing my decisions. In that way, my overseas adventure could not have been better timed. Food, wine, and international reporting became my prescription for self-care.

"I don't care what else happens in my career at NBC," I remember thinking, long before my first bite of squid ink pasta that night in Venice. "I will be forever grateful that they sent me here."

And Venice was just the beginning.

I flew to Rotterdam next, where I stayed at a hotel that looked like a Wes Anderson set. I still fantasize about the breakfast spread, a continental offering of cured meats, hard cheeses, and boiled eggs. The olives looked biblical, which was appropriate for a story about a guy who built a full-scale replica of Noah's Ark out of beech wood, then stocked it with real animals. Goats. Ponies. Peacocks. Even kangaroos.

Back in America, this would be a familiar kind of quest story. But overseas, everything had a new shine. When I asked about the kangaroos, I was told that people donate them to the Ark because "otherwise they make hamburgers of them."

News to me.

Near the end of my ten-day stint in London, as I confronted the fact that I couldn't run forever, a plane disappeared on its way from Kuala Lumpur to Beijing. That set off a chain of phone calls that ended with a buzzing device in my pocket. I had four hours to catch a flight to equatorial Southeast Asia—thirteen hours away from London, across so many time zones that I landed a disorienting thirteen hours *ahead* of the local time in New York. I was scheduled to appear on the *Today* show almost immediately. Or was it *Nightly News*? It would take me days to get the time zones straight.

The main course of overseas coverage is crisis and tragedy. It's a jarring double vision for a foreign correspondent, shuttling between not only two worlds but two kinds of experience. A part of you is excited to explore a new country. But wherever you go is—almost by definition of you being there to cover it—a living nightmare, one of the saddest, most contested, or otherwise ugliest places on the planet at that moment, even if it's also still one of the most beautiful.

I arrived in Kuala Lumpur to silent prayer vigils for the victims and viciously unhelpful press conferences. How could a jet with 239 passengers and crew on board just disappear into the wind in the twenty-first century? No country involved wanted to talk about their radar capabilities: what they knew or didn't know. Malaysia, meanwhile, didn't want to admit that everyone on board was probably dead.

Days went by, then weeks. I'd work until my nerves were shot and by night—or when it was night in America, anyway—I'd explore, occupying my mind anyway I could. Mosques. Holy sites. I ordered food from stalls lit by buzzing fluorescent lights, then ate on plastic stools, my plate cradling dishes with names I couldn't pronounce and ingredients I'd never tried. I nearly burned off my taste buds with flavor.

Back at the hotel, I found two new diversions. I watched K-pop TV and tried to figure out the toilet. I was staying at a Hilton unlike any Hilton back home. In the bathroom there was a smart toilet, the R2-D2 of porcelain thrones. I'm not exaggerating. It sensed me when I walked in, the lid opening as if in greeting. I peered over it and pressed one of the buttons on the wall. A jet of water shot directly up and into my dumb face.

"I'm not sure what I expected," I said to no one but the toilet.

It was a bidet button.

After two weeks, the story moved south and I did too.

The cause of the disappearance was still utterly unknown, but an international team of investigators guessed that the plane had most likely gone down in the Indian Ocean. Perth, Australia, was the closest city, so that's where I headed. Perth is the most isolated big city in the world. The same $8 bottle of nail polish you'd buy in New York costs $17 there.

For me, though, the shock of Perth was the familiarity. It felt like California without the people and the development, which made it feel like California in an alternate dimension. The whole country smelled like the eucalyptus trees I used to swing on as a kid, only bigger, with an aura of something ancient and wild.

I threw myself into the story, but that scent always pointed my thoughts back toward home. For the first time in weeks, I found myself daydreaming about my childhood, my father, our fights and our feuds. From so many thousands of miles away, your decisions take on a distant, almost alien quality, like they were made by someone else. I found myself wondering if I'd done it all wrong with my family. Maybe I never should have left California. Maybe I should have stayed and tended to my father, stepped into the vacant roles of my mother or grandmother.

What is my responsibility to my father? How much should I sacrifice? Or suffer? On what grounds? By what theory? I didn't know. The question of when to leave is the one that haunts me. Some will say, of course you had to go. You had to save yourself. Others will say, no, you had to stay. Nothing is more important than family.

I took a run to clear my head, but the fog only deepened and the next thing I knew I was on the ground, bleeding into the sidewalk, writhing in pain. I'd fallen. I have no idea how, but I'd heard something tear—maybe a tendon. From the ground, in tears, I called my cameraman, who had spent the last decade or more covering war zones. He scooped me up and rushed me to the emergency room.

The doctors told me to pick up a jug of water. It sent a bolt of pain through my shoulder so strong I had to sit down. I hadn't broken a thing, it turned out, but a break might have been less painful. I had a bruise so deep, and ligaments so strained, I had to wear a sling for weeks.

It became a joke on television.

"We see that you have a little arm sling on," said Carson Daly on the *Today* show the next day. "We understand you had a jogging accident yesterday, wishing you a speedy recovery."

"I'm not good at exercising apparently. Thank you, though," I said.

Brian Williams had his own spin that evening.

"Katy Tur, who I should mention, has a busted wing," he said after I tossed back to him in the studio. "Our thanks to the Australian ER docs for patching up the visiting American."

After fifty days and three continents, I felt more or less patched up emotionally as well. Or at least I was ready to try again. I boarded a flight back to America, and back into a relationship with my father.

———

By the summer of 2014, we hadn't seen each other in over a year but we were emailing and texting. I was still angry, and hurt (and so was she, no doubt), but I pushed it aside and offered my support. She seemed to accept it. Her transition plan had changed, she told me, as she adjusted to setbacks with insurance that wouldn't cover her or therapists who thought she might be moving too fast. But in July she texted me a smiling post-op photo from Thailand.

"I'm a bouncing baby girl!" she said.

I congratulated her and told her she looked great. I asked her how she was feeling and what she planned to do next. I told her I was excited for her and it was true. I knew the suicide statistics for trans people. In fact, she sent them to me one day out of the blue— a distressing sign. I wrote back immediately.

"Are you considering commuting suicide?" I asked, misspelling "committing."

"No," she said, seeing an opening for a little joke. "I never commute while dead."

I decided to play along.

"Good, I hear the highway is hell."

"I've never been happier," she declared.

And it seemed to be true.

She tweeted about getting stuck in a blouse in a changing room, which, as someone who has gotten stuck in a blouse in many changing rooms, I found relatable. She also posted an experimental shot of her nipple (removed by Facebook, allowed by Twitter) and selfies with Leica. I cringed a little as she continued talking about her smaller, more feminine brain and her newfound interest in consensus building. The lady jokes didn't end either. In fact, they multiplied.

"Apologies to all women in my life for taking time to get ready," she tweeted after her surgery. "The endless purse searches. Being female is work! Lookin 4 handyman!"

But all in all, both of us seemed to be going in a good direction. In September, we reconnected by phone. We didn't make peace, but we agreed to keep speaking.

I also decided to keep moving.

I loved working overseas. When you're a journalist in America you get to take one piece of the global pie. When you are a foreign correspondent, covering the world, the rest of the pie is yours. It meant that at any moment, I could be called to go anywhere, which, in this moment, I found appetizing.

When the network asked me if I wanted to move to London, I didn't think twice.

"Send me now!" I said.

That November I ran through my final checklist for London. I was going to be a full-time NBC News foreign correspondent. All these years later, it's still fun to write those words into a sentence: Katy Tur, NBC News foreign correspondent. I packed my bags and put everything I couldn't carry into a shipping container. I also applied for and got two passports. Yes, *two*. Both of them real. Both of them for the United States. Both of them legal. I needed them for a ho-hum paperwork reason: I might, for example, need to use one to apply for a visa while also traveling on the other one. It felt exhilarating. I was told to ask for extra pages in my second passport. It will fill up fast, a colleague said. I hoped they were right.

I also had to get shots. A lot of shots. A special yellow immunization card that would prepare me for sudden travel into any disease vector on the planet. But the hardest part of my preparation was HEAT training. HEAT is an acronym for hostile environment awareness training. Kidnappings. Bombings. Violent crime. Terrorist plots. A three-day session outside the city, run by former special operations types, mostly from overseas. It's supposed to prepare you for the worst. You won't be Jason Bourne with a reporter's notepad, but you might not die. That's the idea, anyway. And it's real, or as close to real as the insurance companies will allow, a "high fidelity" model.

I learned how to avoid problems. Dress in plain clothes, loose-fitting, sneakers or boots, nothing showy, no jewelry or watches, or anything that looks like money. Then I learned how to help if things get bloody. How to apply a tourniquet. How to do CPR. How to dress a bullet wound. Finally, they bring you outside and run you through scenarios.

You get in a van and pull up to a checkpoint. A bunch of guys run out, guns drawn, faces covered in scarves. You make it through, but at the next one you're told to get out and run. And even though you know you're on the grounds of a Girl Scout camp, you run like hell, ducking and diving behind the best protection you can find. And we learned what that was. Cinder block for some guns. A vehicle's engine block for others. A thick tree if nothing is around.

But it doesn't work. You don't escape. At some point in the scenario, you're kidnapped, blindfolded, bound, and pushed to your knees. The instructors blast Metallica to menace and disorientate you, but you can still hear your classmates being dragged away, and eventually you are too.

I landed in London feeling ready, even if the first few weeks of my life overseas were anything but hostile. My flat in London was inside a postcard-worthy little white and brick Georgian row house in Angel. It had flower boxes and shutters, a little square of patio on top of the covered entryway. It wasn't lavish, but deeply livable with a small guest bedroom that I turned into a large closet.

There was a lot of fun in London. The bureau was full of young expats from this place or that. Most of us single and childless. We were united by a certain sense of thievery, a feeling like we were stealing moments never meant for us to experience. We'd drop in on lives and worlds we had nothing to do with, then retreat as if never there.

There was cheap glamour too. After the first two hours of the *Today* show aired, at the very reasonable local hour of 2 p.m., a coworker and I would go to lunch which more often than not included a glass of wine. In the afternoon for a midday break, we'd get tea with biscuits, which is just the fancy British way of saying cookie. On Fridays, the meet-up place for the building's weekly fire drill was a pub down the road, which obviously had a great happy hour.

And then there was the champagne. The bottles and bottles and bottles of champagne. Or at least Prosecco. You were always served a glass of bubbly first at a social event. When I started having my own parties I'd judge their success based on the number of bottles I had piled up in my kitchen the next morning. I think the record was nineteen. About the same number of partygoers.

I only rarely thought of home.

———

One of my first assignments as a permanent member of the NBC London bureau was the tenth anniversary of the Indian Ocean tsunami. We flew in to find the spirit of renewal you hope for in a story like this one. An earthquake had sent a thirty-foot wave toward the coasts of Indonesia, Sri Lanka, India, the Maldives, and Thailand, sweeping nearly a quarter-million people to their death.

The loss in Indonesia alone was north of 200,000 people, most of them in the Aceh province of Sumatra. There we met the same local guide—a so-called fixer—who worked with Brian Williams and his NBC team in the immediate aftermath back in 2004.

He said that NBC had been good to him and his family, a blessing amid the catastrophe. In return, he welcomed us back and asked us to be the honored guests at his daughter's wedding. We accepted, grateful and flattered. In a picture from that day, I'm barefoot on an immaculate rug with my hair wrapped in a scarf. Behind me is a shrine of gold and green, outlined in red. To my left in the center of the picture are the newlyweds themselves—in full golden regalia, modern-day royals. The whole immediate family is in the picture, dressed for celebration. It's a picture of peace.

The same day as the wedding, I got a text from a friend back home. *Los Angeles* magazine had just published an eight-thousand-word feature on my father, titled "Becoming Zoey." I clicked on the link and up popped a shot of my father in a black dress, coyly looking down, hands running through her now shoulder-length blond hair. My father used to say she believed in burning the ship after crossing the Rubicon. That way you have no choice but to stay and make it in the New World. I was happy to see that old adage had served her well. No regrets, all joy, blue skies ahead.

Parts of the article felt like time travel, a chance for me to float into the past. I knew about the abuse in my father's childhood, for example, but not the yearning. When my dad's mother bought a new refrigerator, Zoey said she played with the box, imagining a machine that could transform boys into girls. When she saw the movie *Georgy Girl*, she fell in love with the title song, which sounded to her like a song about transitioning. "There's another Georgy deep inside / Bring out all the love you hide and, oh, what a change there'd be / The world would see a new Georgy Girl."

I learned that the father I knew, the Bob Tur macho newsman, had been an act, an elaborate fiction. That her whole career as a gonzo reporter was a strange kind of comfort, almost a balm or at least a welcome alternative to the pain within. I also learned new details about the run-up to the call my father made to me in Boston, the big announcement of a change to come.

She had taken a portrait with Leica that was supposed to double as a farewell. She said she'd been thinking about it for a long time, but now she had a clear plan. She had the place. She had the method. And she even put herself into position to go through with it. But that morning at 2 a.m., another solution presented itself.

"I just broke down," Zoey told the reporter. "I said out loud, 'I want to be a woman. I want to be a woman. I'm so terrible at being a guy.'"

It might have been my distance (in Banda Aceh), or the people I was surrounded by (survivors of a terrible disaster), or my own guilt at not being some better, warmer, more devoted and doting daughter all these years. But the more I learned about the transition, the more I wanted to tell my father that it was all going to be okay.

Then I got to a section I'd been dreading. The reporter had called me ahead of time to get comment, so I knew it was coming. My father was describing our relationship and my reaction to the transition. "Classic Katy," my father had called it. "She took it well. It was, 'I can't believe this, my dad wants to be a woman.' Then it stopped being funny."

Funny? What was she talking about?

In her version of events, I had rejected her and made her feel like a "nonperson."

"I didn't kill anyone. I didn't hurt anybody," she said. "Even sociopaths go to court and have their families sitting next to them, but God forbid you want to be a woman."

I rejected *her*? I made *her* feel like a nonperson? Like a murderer or a sociopath? She must have known this wasn't true since I had told her over and over again what I needed. In her early interviews she had acknowledged it as well. So what changed?

I was hurt and betrayed by my father's comments but also worried. Instead of talking to me, her daughter, she seemed to want to fight with me, the public figure, through the press. I knew what she wanted, or I thought I knew: a public declaration of love and forgiveness. I wasn't willing to offer one, not without a private discussion about pain and abuse.

Her words were not explicitly hostile, but I heard them in the context of history, and I found myself afraid. I thought of my mother, telling me not to let my father know where she lived. I was thousands of miles away, but worried my father might come find me.

I spent New Year's in Indonesia and hoped 2015 would be a better year for us.

CHAPTER EIGHT

"Zis Ees Not What We Do en France"

I could hide in Paris.

I was still working out of the London bureau for NBC, but a friend and I had decided to try a novel way of weekending through Europe. I'd read an article that said the best way to live like a local was to land, find your own place (this was key), and then log onto Tinder. In theory, you'd end up on dates with local guys, doing local things, and experience a new city like a native. What the hell, I thought. I was a single lady in my early thirties. Let's try it in Paris, I said. My friend was game

Over dinner, I found the profile of a smiley brown-haired guy with a thick five o'clock shadow wearing a tailored button-down white shirt. I'll admit the shirt looked a little too tight, but he was French. He was also cute but there are lots of cute guys out there. What clinched it was the microphone clipped to his lapel in one of his profile pictures. There was a camera in another shot. He's a TV guy, I realized. "He can't be an axe murderer if he's on TV," I told my friend.

He messaged me back, in broken English, and that very night we all met up at a Parisian club. A few drinks later I was making out with him on the dance floor to Sia's "Chandelier."

Party girls don't get hurt, right?

I was trying my best. We said goodbye at closing time.

"A bientôt, Kat-tee," he said as I was walking away.

"Huh?"

"You don't know à bientôt? You must know à bientôt. Zis ees Paris."

"All right, what does it mean?"

"Eet means, see you soon."

I told him that's nice but my train back to London was leaving in the morning. He told me he'd come say goodbye. I laughed.

"Sure," I said. "It leaves at ten."

I was confident I would not be seeing this Benoit guy again. But you know what? I found him standing at the top of the single escalator that leads to the boarding gates. He was holding his scooter helmet and smiling at me with a good thirty minutes to spare.

"I told you I wanted to say goodbye," he said.

We kissed and made plans to see each other again the following weekend. Before long, I had a French boyfriend.

It was his place I could hide in, a studio apartment in the 14th arrondissement. The bed in a loft, connected to the living area by a black iron spiral staircase. I climbed down and tiptoed to the kitchen. In America, I would have made a giant cup of coffee but "filter coffee," as the Europeans call it, is considered to be a sin and a spell-breaker, here in France. I popped a little espresso pod into a sleek French machine.

This was my routine on almost every weekend in the first half of 2015. I sipped my espresso and stared down into the courtyards, through a giant wall of windows, each panel of glass the size of a dining room table. I could see the neighbors as they chatted over breakfast. I could see gray tile roofs and smokestacks. Rooflines as iconic as the Eiffel Tower but better because this was the real Paris.

I always woke up before Benoit, hoping the smell of espresso would finally rouse him. Eventually it did.

"You're lazy and French," I'd say, when he came down, hoping to get a flirty rise out of him. It always worked.

"You're American and you are too much in a rush," he'd volley back in broken syntax.

My routine was to turn on French TV and laugh along with *Le Petit Journal*, France's version of *The Daily Show*. Even though I understood precisely 3 percent of the dialogue, I'd crack up anyway, and if the scent of espresso didn't wake him, my laughter would.

"It's nine a.m.!" I'd say. "I'm hungry."

"Allons au marché!"

"In English, please!"

"Mais, Katy, you need to learn French."

"Pff," was my only response. "I know 'pff.' That's enough."

Our days were one watercolor painting after another. The farmer's market. Fish on ice. Bright green lettuce. Small red strawberries. Eggs for breakfast. A scooter ride to Parc Montsouris. We'd collapse on a grassy patch. No blankets. No plans. An entire country with a ban on email after work.

On the way home, we'd stop at a café for cheese and bread and a bottle of rosé. More often than not, Benoit's friends would join us for another bottle, this time along the banks of the Grand Canal. Whatever you think of when you think of French romance, this was it and more.

I'd gone from L.A. to New York, then New York to London,

and now London to Paris, but whatever was going on with my dad still found me.

———

In February of 2015, my father grabbed a microphone and climbed back into a news helicopter. It was like old times, as she lifted off from Orange County and swept over downtown Los Angeles, showing off the same confidence in the cockpit that first made her famous as a pilot. She was narrating it all for *Inside Edition*, which had just announced her as a Special Correspondent and "America's first transgender TV news correspondent." My mom cooperated in a little reunion for the package, suffering through bad jokes about how—since Zoey's transition—people have wondered if that makes her a lesbian.

I felt bad for her. No matter what was happening in her life, no matter how far she distanced herself from my dad. Not the divorce, not her new boyfriend, not the decade since they stopped living together could separate her from my dad. She kept getting called back to be a character in my father's show. I wondered why she kept saying yes.

But she did and not only that, she kept trying to help mend the break between my father and me. She kept me updated on all of my dad's news, including this new job. I felt a familiar wave of trepidation but it was a new year and I wanted a fresh start on whatever terms we could find.

"Congratulations!" I texted from London. "You look great in that first segment—very beautiful."

But still in that same appearance—her first television interview since the transition—my father burned me publicly. She said I was outright struggling with the idea of my dad as a woman. The comment seemed calculated to ride a national wave of vitriol over trans rights, which made my issues with my transgender father more than just a family matter. Some headlines put me squarely on the side of the bad guys who are afraid of trans people. I am not.

"Transgender newscaster Zoey Tur reveals NBC correspondent daughter Katy stopped speaking to her after decision to have a sex change," blared the *Daily Mail*.

She made similar comments everywhere she went, as though I were the one who'd stormed out of our last dinner and said "you're disgusting" and "I never want to see you again."

I hated my dad when I read that. It reminded me of the time Dad called me "as self-absorbed as can be without resembling a black hole." Or that time on my birthday, when she wished me the best "on another year of the sun revolving around you." She was always taking shots. And they hurt.

I went to Paris to keep ducking them, or to try to. I went to ignore the headlines and the tweets, to live a separate life in another land, a place where no one knew my dad, or me, or cared about hot-button issues in America. Yeah, I still followed the coverage, glanced at it through the steam of my morning espresso. But to read it from France was like scanning the earth from the International Space Station. Sometimes you can see the smoke from fires, but you know the flames will never reach you.

Throughout early 2015, my father wasn't only fast and loose with the facts around our personal relationship. She went on HLN and CNN and TMZ and performed the conversational equivalent of a drunk dancing her way through a room of trip wires and fine porcelain. The damage was extensive, the bill was huge.

She suggested that "male puberty" be a possible cutoff point for trans kids in youth sports, which may sound reasonable enough and is a popular talking point on the right. But youth sports are for youths. Don't all kids deserve the right to play?

She said that hormone therapy very often changed a person's sexual orientation. In other words, if a man takes estrogen, all else equal, my father said that man will start finding other men attractive. ("It's really strange, but hormones, you know?")

Her source was a single unpublished, preliminary study. It was like reading a health claim on a random bottle of pills in a vitamin store and then stating it as accepted fact on national television.

Her biggest faceplants were on major pieces of national news. A woman at Planet Fitness complained that a trans woman was using the changing room. The woman spent days warning other members of this open locker room policy, growing so vocal that Planet Fitness revoked the complainer's membership. Enter my father, who said people have a right to be concerned. My dad speculated that the trans woman in question might "perv out on women." She thought everyone should have a private changing room.

Finally, there was Caitlyn Jenner, former Olympian, current Kardashian stepparent, one of the most famous people—in one of the most famous families—on the planet. By 2015, Caitlyn's appearance was changing and there were rumors that she might be on the brink of coming out as a trans woman. She eventually did in April. But my father outed Caitlyn in February! Twice!

GLAAD wrote a letter of complaint to CNN about my dad's segment. *The Advocate* wrote a blow-by-blow account of how my dad's contract at *Inside Edition* wasn't extended, listing the different complaints from all the different advocacy groups about what my dad was saying. In response, my dad told *The Advocate* that she was being silenced and that the effort amounted to violence against women.

"I was told by two major LGBT advocate groups that I should sit down, shut up, and listen," she told *The Advocate*. "I was told like I'm a stupid woman. That's violence, terrible violence, to tell a woman to sit down and shut up."

Inside Edition said the job was always going to be just a month long.

I never said a word of any of this to Benoit, only sparingly brought it up to my colleagues in London. In fact, the only time I ever mentioned my father was to tell my colleagues not to let her know where I lived. Again, I couldn't explain why exactly but for some reason I felt like my mom did when she first left my dad.

It's fine, I told myself.

I was never coming home.

"Do you know the story of the Zen master and the little boy?"

Toward the end of *Charlie Wilson's War*, this is how a character—a CIA officer played by Philip Seymour Hoffman—introduces a little fable about the risks of drawing conclusions too soon. It's one of my favorite scenes in any movie and it goes like this.

The boy's father bought him a horse for his fourteenth birthday and everyone in the village said, "Isn't that wonderful, the boy got a horse?"

The Zen master said, "We'll see."

A couple of years later the boy fell from his horse, badly breaking his leg, and everyone in the village said, "How awful, he won't be able to walk properly."

The Zen master said, "We'll see."

Then, a war broke out and all the young men had to go and fight, but this young man couldn't because his leg was still messed up and everyone said, "How wonderful!"

The Zen master said, "We'll see."

This is how I feel about every twist and turn in my father's story and my own. At times, she has felt like a curse. Other times, she has felt like a blessing. I can thank my father for training me, pushing me, shaping me as a reporter and broadcaster. I can hate her for hitting me, slapping me, chasing me, hurting my mother and brother, kicking my dog, and burning down our lives. But my father's role in my life is not good or bad or both or neither. It's everything. And it's nothing.

Because the story is always still unfolding.

———

The rumblings of the rest of your life always seem to start without you knowing it.

In my case, the headlines really were headlines, but I was missing them. I wasn't ignoring them. It's not like I was sitting overseas in London not reading the newspapers and turning the channel whenever the future was on. I was paying attention to everything, just not American politics.

If you'd asked me about Ted Cruz, I'd have assumed you meant Tom Cruise. If you showed me a picture of Bernie Sanders, I'd be impressed Larry David got such a striking look-alike for his biopic. I might have been able to tell you Hillary Clinton was planning to run, or running, or "exploring" a run—but that's about it. Okay I'm exaggerating but I'm trying to make a point. The *Game of Thrones* for the Oval Office was not my beat.

I certainly didn't know that Donald Trump had hired a what's-his-name campaign manager, borrowed a communications director from his daughter Ivanka, and descended the Trump Tower escalators with his third wife, Melania. I didn't know he'd ditched his prepared remarks, ad-libbing his way into a few now familiar campaign talking points. I didn't even know about those eight infamous sentences, tossed off two minutes into his announcement, the ones that got him in so much trouble.

"When Mexico sends its people, they're not sending their best.

They're not sending you. They're not sending you. They're send-ing people that have lots of problems, and they're bringing those problems with us. They're bringing drugs. They're bringing crime. They're rapists. And some, I assume, are good people."

I had missed it, busy reporting from the rubble of an earthquake in Nepal or on the wreckage of a downed passenger jet in Ukraine or on exorcisms in the foothills of the Swiss Alps. I was captivated by my new life, so much so I told my cameraman that I would never leave my job in London. There's nothing NBC can do to get me to go back, I said. I'm going to be a foreign correspondent forever.

Also: I was planning a vacation.

In just two weeks, I intended to be on a big, fat ripe tomato of a tour around Sicily with my scooter-riding French boyfriend. I'd be on beaches with striped umbrellas, having drinks with spritz in the name, and eating an obscene amount of pasta. I'd spent my year traveling, but almost none of it vacationing. There's a difference. I was ready to do nothing—with purpose. I needed it.

But the rumblings were there, and, by coincidence, I was on my way back to New York.

The Make-A-Wish Foundation had asked me to bring a sick teenage boy named Aaron along on a story for a day. Of course, I said, and we'd settled on June as the best time to do it. By then I'd been established enough in London to feel okay with taking a break from the bureau and absent enough in New York to want to remind the network bosses I existed. I booked a ticket to New York, left clothes in the dryer and milk in the fridge of my flat in London, and told Benoit I'd meet him on vacation in Sicily in two weeks.

It was a great time to be in New York City. The Supreme Court had just handed down its decision to legalize gay marriage, and thousands of happy people were gathered to celebrate at the Stonewall Inn, birthplace of the LGBTQ movement. I brought Aaron and his family along with me. I also thought of my father as a child feeling like a little girl. This was a victory for her too, I marveled at how accepting this country had become, how love had won. The future looked blazingly bright.

I said goodbye to Aaron and his family outside the neon signs that announce NBC STUDIOS and went upstairs to loiter in the *Nightly News* offices. I had no plan, no purpose. My only ambition was to hover and chitchat and see what would happen.

———

The Trump outrage had built to such a point that NBC needed a reporter to cover it for a few days and I became that reporter. I was drafted into service by a shout and point.

"How about Katy?" someone had said. "She's just standing around."

I would go on to write an entire book about the experience, an unexpected bestseller by an unexpected campaign correspondent about an unexpected run to the White House. No one could quite explain what the hell had just happened, but everyone seemed to notice the dynamic between me and Trump.

When I went on *The Daily Show* to promote my book in 2017, the host, Trevor Noah, felt his way to an unusual question for a campaign reporter. "It almost felt like there was a strange connection between yourself and Donald Trump," he said. I remember it was a weird question but I knew why he asked and I knew the answer.

"Did you feel it?" he asked.

Yeah, I felt it, but I dodged the question because the answer would have only raised more questions. Before the campaign, I'd never met and barely followed Trump's career. But from that first day on the campaign trail, I felt a deep familiarity. It was like I already knew him.

———

"Katy Tur, you're not paying attention!"

I was at my first official Trump event, a last-minute assignment, and I was standing in the backyard of a house in New Hampshire. It was lightly raining and I was dressed in a ridiculous low-cut pink dress that was the closest thing I had to appropriate for a political event. I wrapped a shawl around my shoulders for modesty and warmth and waited for the candidate to appear.

Finally, a kid in an ill-fitting suit introduced the future president to an audience of a couple of hundred overdressed people with umbrellas around a pool. Trump joked about his hair getting rained on. Then he launched into a speech focused on his unparalleled ability to run the country. The crowd cheered. Then Trump paused and took a turn toward me personally.

"Here's my only problem. When television, I mean, these people," he said. "I mean, Katy hasn't even looked up once at me . . ."

How did he know my name? I figured he must have recognized me from my days at NBC's local New York station. But why was he looking right at me and why was he calling me out?

"I'm tweeting what you're saying!" I yelled back.

Trump considered my excuse for a moment and nodded approvingly.

"I hope so," he said. "I think you do a good job, by the way Katy."

Later, on my drive back to New York, I thought about that moment some more. I thought there was supposed to be a certain formality between politicians and reporters. You say, "Mister," or "Senator," or begin your questions with "Respectfully." I didn't consider the "respectfully" line until I heard another reporter say it to Ted Cruz, months into the campaign. Ooh, that's good, I thought. But with Trump the feeling was different. He called me out in a crowd, suggested I was doing something wrong and disrespectful. But instead of feeling embarrassed or apologetic I felt absolute calm.

I'd dealt with this kind of behavior before. This insistence on attention. This love of coverage and publicity, no matter how good or bad. This obsession with respect and tolerance for fighting and feuding. I recognized the mix of victimhood and outrage, the how-could-yous and how-dare-yous—because I'd seen it all before in my own family. My father is not Donald Trump and Donald Trump is not my father. But if anyone asked me, I'd recommend the same therapist.

———

"How'd you like to spend the summer in New York?"

That question, lobbed over to me by NBC's head of newsgathering that same day, was why I'd ended up in New Hampshire. He asked me as he headed toward the elevators, no doubt on his way to a more important meeting. NBC already had six brilliant political reporters, covering all the most viable candidates. Neither Trump nor I were in that initial mix.

"It will be six weeks, tops," he said, pausing at the doors. "But hey, if he wins, you'll go to the White House."

We both laughed.

I said sure even though I knew it meant the end of my Sicilian vacation.

I said sure because I'd remembered a conversation from my first trip to London, to cover the Olympics in 2012.

I was working for WNBC, in New York, and I went for drinks

with some people from the network. One round led to another, which led to me sitting on a stool in the bar of our not-at-all-glamorous hotel for business travelers. On the stool next to me was a veteran of the business with the scars to show it. She said:

"Let me tell you what your life is going to be like: You're not going to have one. Forget dinner plans. Forget dating. Forget marriage. Forget children. They're going to send you to stories in the middle of the night, for days at a time, and you'll never know when you'll be coming home."

She was divorced and had no children and from where she was sitting she was also totally right about the business. I can imagine how the conversation must have seemed from her perspective. Here I was, late twenties, excited about a big new job, and totally clueless about what I was giving up. I imagine she thought she was doing me a favor, making sure I had my eyes open as I took the leap.

But I just wanted to shut them and cry. And so I did. I fled to my room, called my mother, and bawled my eyes out for hours. But you know what? From that day on, I lived much the life she said I would. I chose my career over my life. And you know what else? I loved every second of it.

So after the rally in New Hampshire, I FaceTimed Benoit.

"Tu me manques," I said in my shitty French. "Mais . . ."

I didn't know the words so I blurted it out in English.

"I have to stay in America. I don't know for how long. I can't come to Sicily."

"Mais, Katy. You are a foreign correspondent," he said pronouncing correspondent like fondant on a cake. "Zis ees not what we do en France." I could hear the anger in his voice. But his anger annoyed me. This was my job. I can't say no to my bosses. I can't tell them I don't want the opportunity. Who knows where it could lead?

119

In July I had my first sit-down interview with Trump.

It didn't feel combative in the moment, but when I got back to the office everyone else was in shock. I kept getting asked about it, pulled aside, queried. "That was a really tense interview," someone said. "Did you not feel it?"

"No," I said. "It felt totally normal to me."

It was only later, when I watched it back on air that I saw what everyone else had seen.

He wanted to shame me. Intimidate me. Talk down to me. He cut me off and called me "naïve" at one point. When I flubbed a line, he said: "Try getting it out! You don't even know what you're talking about."

But tense? No. It didn't feel tense. I was Brer Rabbit getting tossed in the briar patch. It felt like home. Looking back, this interview was Donald Trump in full: inaccurate, bullying, and shameless. Nothing would change him, I thought, and nothing did.

Fate got me the assignment. Dumb devotion to work made me say yes. But my ability to stick with the Trump beat, to stay on the job—fending off competition and fatigue and buckets of abuse, to hang around long enough to watch the country change, and with it my little life—all of it goes back to my father.

A week after my Trump sit-down, Zoey Tur had a tense public sit-down of her own. She was appearing on *Dr. Drew on Call*, a late-night show on HLN. She was part of a panel to discuss whether Caitlyn Jenner was worthy of an ESPY Arthur Ashe Courage Award. Was courage really on display in her decision to come out as a rich, white, famous, former Olympian who is also transgender?

One of the panelists, an entertainment journalist, argued no, she does not deserve a courage award. She is brave for coming out, but courage is a word reserved for the people who fought back at Stonewall, pushed for gay liberation and equal rights. Movement people, not media people.

My father responded by managing to take all sides of the issue and boast at the same time.

"Does she deserve it? Probably not. Is she brave? Of course she's brave," my father said. "To come out as transgender is horribly difficult. It is the most difficult thing you can do. I've been overseas. I've flown helicopter missions, surveillance missions. I've been shot, stabbed. Being brave is being yourself and being transgender is about the bravest thing you can do. Does she deserve it? Of course she deserves it."

My father paused as though expecting an eruption of applause from the studio audience, but the conversation turned.

Ben Shapiro (then a Breitbart editor-at-large) stepped in to troll the whole show.

"Why are we mainstreaming delusion?" he said. "Facts don't care about your feelings. It turns out that every chromosome, every cell in Caitlyn Jenner's body, is male, with the exception of some of his sperm cells. It turns out that he still has all of his male appendages. How he feels on the inside is irrelevant to the question of his biological self."

My father sat tall in a purple dress with black leather piping. Ben Shapiro sat to her left, wearing a pink shirt with a striped tie under a suit jacket and Jewish kippah.

My father cut in.

"We both know chromosomes don't necessarily mean you're male or female," she said.

Her voice took on a singsong quality I knew like the bell before the blades start spinning on a giant saw. She turned to Shapiro and put her hand on his shoulder. They turned toward one another.

"You don't know what you're talking about," she said, the alarm bell rising and rising. "You're not educated on genetics."

Shapiro couldn't hear it or didn't care.

He looked at my father: "What are your genetics, sir?"

While the camera cut away to Dr. Drew, I could see my father's face in my mind's eye. When the camera found her again, she was doing exactly what I feared. She grabbed Shapiro's neck, the fingers of her left hand visible on the far left side of Shapiro's collar. Then in a low, hard voice she said:

"You cut that out now, or you'll go home in an ambulance."

Shapiro filed a police report.

Worse, in a cultural sense, anyone opposed to rights and acceptance for the trans community might now point to my father as a reason—as proof that trans people were unstable or dangerous. Of course, I knew otherwise. My father's rage had nothing to do with her transition. It was not a moment of truth about the trans community but a moment of consistency from my father—who in becoming her true self remained exactly who she always was.

As it turned out, this episode was also a preview of the next eighteen months (to maybe eighteen years) in America. Shapiro's police report was political theater, a prompt for another round of headlines and views, a push to keep the story trending on Facebook and Twitter. Outrage poured in from all sides. Then when reached for comment by the *Los Angeles Times*, my father doubled down on her behavior in the most emotional language I can imagine.

"I reacted like any woman would react," she said. "If some guy is calling you mentally ill and calling you 'Sir' you wouldn't like it. You would be upset by it. And yet, I am supposed to take it because if I don't take it, I am not being ladylike. I'm finding that to be a lady, you must accept being told to sit down, shut up and listen."

Then Shapiro did the same thing, calling my father's comments a case of illegal bullying and blaming the writer and the media at large. "Your willingness, and the media's more general willingness, to ignore that basic standard of decency and civilization out of sympathy for those who violate such standards is repulsive," he said.

Dad once again on the cutting edge of the oncoming political storm.

CHAPTER NINE

"I Hear You Have a Crazy Father Too"

I was in New York in August of 2015, getting done up for an MSNBC hit when I looked at the television and saw a new face. I turned to Barbara and Mary, the makeup artists:

"Who is *that*?" I said. "Does he work here? How come I don't know him?"

Makeup artists are the information pipeline of any news organization. They know everyone and everything.

"Oh, that's Tony," said Mary. "We all have a crush on Tony."

"How do I not know him? He's so hot!"

"He's a writer for digital, I think. He has a streaming show too, something about the environment. He's very cute."

Very cute, indeed.

Al Sharpton was interviewing him about pollution in the Colorado River. Or at least that's what the banner said. The TV was on mute. I stared at the screen. Thick head of brown hair, check, strong jaw, check, ill-fitting yet scholarly blazer, check, glasses, check.

He looked like a writer and I have long had a thing for writers, or for intellectuals with a little brawn thrown in. I remember watching Indiana Jones as he scaled a broken dusty rope ladder, forearms flexed and glistening, glasses and university offices just a few scenes back. I felt like Tony could climb a rope ladder.

With my face half-done, my hair in a pile of curlers, Tony walked into the makeup room, right up next to me. He reached for a makeup wipe, shook it out full, put it over his face and started rubbing aggressively in a move that screamed NOT A TV PERSON. TV makeup is thick, it needs to be taken off in layers, particularly if you have any hopes of saving your skin from looking twenty years older than it actually is.

"Tony, have you met Katy?" Jenaii, another stylist, blurted out, forcing an interaction.

My face started burning.

"Uhh no," Tony said, giving me a quick glance. "But you're following Trump, right? I saw your sit-down. Crazy stuff. Nice to meet you."

I sat there in stunned silence. Yes, he was handsome. Yes, he looked like a writer and, according to Mary, actually was one. But there was something more. A certain sadness. I remember wanting to see him smile.

A few days later, he followed me on Twitter late at night and I took it as a good sign. To play it cool I didn't follow him back until the next day. But no message from him ever came. No "hey, nice to meet you." No "hey, let's get a drink sometime." No "hey" at all.

In the interim I'd done a little googling and stumbled upon an online video report he'd done about . . . Styrofoam. New York was about to ban Styrofoam, to the cheers of many, but the video was Tony's tongue-in-cheek ode to the stuff.

The joy of getting a soda in a Styrofoam cup with crushed ice. The pleasure of a hot cocoa to go. The feeling of packing and unpacking. At one point in the report, he emerged from a full box of Styrofoam peanuts, whispering sweet nothings to them.

I decided to take matters into my own hands.

I was in Birch Run, Michigan, covering a Trump rally, one of the last rallies where they sold booze (and therefore one of the last where I saw a woman vomiting into a toilet). It was also one of the first rallies where the other networks started to take Trump seriously. My friend Sara Murray arrived for CNN. The timing was perfect. We spent the entire drive back to the airport gaming out exactly what I would write to Tony. Something not too serious but not too flirty. A note that would leave the door open for him to choose which adventure would come next. This is what we came up with:

"Hey! Confession: I watched your Styrofoam thing online and you made me laugh/want to sleep in a box of Styrofoam peanuts. Want to get a coffee, or Fanta, or frozen daiquiri sometime when I'm not tied to Trump? Katy (from the makeup room)."

I read it and reread it and gathered up my courage. I hit send as the plane was taxiing so by the time it went through, I would already be in the air and unable to obsessively refresh my inbox for a response. The distraction worked. I forgot all about the email until I was already in the car and crossing the Triborough Bridge back to Manhattan.

I checked my email, saw no response, and wrote him off.

As if he could hear me saying, "oh well," my inbox pinged.

He wrote:

"Say, thank you. When the surgeons were done pulling the foam out of my eyebrows, I was really happy with the piece. And I'd love a coffee/Fanta/frozen daiquiri—with preference given to the last option. How's Trump?"

The following Monday we snuck out of work early and got that frozen daiquiri at a bar downtown. I told him about Trump. He told me about his work for digital. He was part of this special long-form unit and had recently done a huge piece on killer commando weathermen, basically gonzo meteorologists who drop into war zones. As part of the reporting he'd gone to Alaska for glacier training. (Very Indiana Jones.)

I started to ask about his family, but I realized I didn't actually need to ask him about his family. I'd seen online that he wrote a whole book about his family. I found a copy of it at the Strand, shelved next to Joan Didion (which I realize is purely alphabetical, but impressive nonetheless). I learned that his father had been one of the biggest marijuana dealers in the United States, selling tons of pot smuggled in on sailboats. In a single job, in 1986, he'd sold enough marijuana to roll a joint for every college-age kid in America. Then he lost it all, failed his family, abused Tony's mom, and haunted Tony's early life. It all sounded so . . . not normal.

I loved the not-normal-ness.

"I hear you have a crazy father too," he said.

It's hard to explain how comforting it felt to hear those eight little words. The dread of explaining myself to new people has stalked me for years. I was tired of talking about helicopters and riots and O.J. and the transition and the fights with my father. My problem is not that people are rude. It's that people are empathetic and interested. They want to know more.

But I just don't want to get into it.

Tony must feel the same way about his own story.

"I do have a crazy father," I said.

And that was that. We started talking about something else.

On our second date, not long after that, we were walking down 14th Street after another round of daiquiris when Tony said he had something to tell me.

Just a few moments before, sitting on barstools inside, we'd shared our first kiss. Tony had almost imperceptibly leaned forward and I had almost imperceptibly held still, which for teenagers of the late nineties and early 2000s is the universal pose of should we kiss/yes, let's. But Tony was a little quiet afterward.

I had a feeling I knew what he was going to tell me. On our first date, he'd left abruptly on a mission that definitely seemed like he had to relieve a babysitter. And then there was the evidence of his desk decorations. Other thirtysomething-year-old guys I knew didn't have cards that said, "I love you more than Batman."

Still, he needed to tell me. And so he did.

"I have two kids."

I nodded.

"I'm gone for the next two weeks because I'm dropping them off in Israel. Their mom is moving there with them."

This I did not know.

"Oh," I said, searching for the right thing to say next. "Are you okay?"

"Yeah. I mean, I think so. It isn't great and I'm not happy about it, but my ex wants to live there and my philosophy is happy parents, happy kids."

"You sure?"

"I don't really have a choice."

"Okay."

He paused. "Listen, I understand if this is a deal-breaker for you."

I looked at him. The sad eyes now made sense. So while yes this was even more complicated than the already significant complication of having two small children, I said it wasn't. There was just something about Tony that felt right. I wasn't willing to walk away from that feeling.

Tony and I kept talking about it all the way back to my hotel. When we stopped to say goodbye, he kissed me again.

"Can I see you when I'm back?" he asked.

"I'd like that," I told him.

"Even though I'm full of dents?"

"Maybe our dents will fit together."

Back in my room my phone pinged. It was a text from Tony. A link to a song by the Happenings called "See You in September."

He did.

The fact of Tony's kids was not a deal-breaker, but it did open the door to another question: What *was* a deal-breaker? I had one in mind, but I wasn't about to raise it. Not yet, anyway. Certainly not on our fourth date. We were at a Japanese restaurant on the Lower East Side. I'd had a few sakes, which probably made me more honest than I might otherwise have been. So when Tony asked me if having kids wasn't a deal-breaker then what would be a deal-breaker, I told him.

I did pause for a moment, first. Wondering if this was the right time to tell him. If the fourth date was maybe a little too soon. But again, I'd had quite a bit of sake, so I went for it.

"A deal-breaker would be if you didn't want any more kids," I said.

Tony's face took on a look of surprise and panic like a guy in a wind tunnel. We hadn't even slept together yet and we were talking about kids.

"You don't have to decide now," I said. "But when you know, or if you know at some point before we get serious, if we get serious, just be honest and tell me."

Tony winced a little. His big concern at that point was not about any possible future children we might have together. It was about the children he already had, the ones now living nearly six thousand miles away. "I need to make sure my children are stable and happy and I have a strong relationship with them," he said. "Until then, I can't think about future kids."

I told him I understood, and we tabled it for the time being, which wasn't so hard. I was still the girl from that barstool in London, warned about what this business can do to your love life, and totally willing to put this whole Tony thing away while I covered the 2016 campaign. I liked the guy, but I wasn't going to give up my shot.

That Halloween, we went to a bar in Queens, where a friend of mine was playing in a drag-themed burlesque show. I'd been on the trail for four months and Trump was attacking the press like no candidate in history. His rallies could feel like a giant rec room, where Trump was throwing popcorn and beer at the TV. And we were the TV. We, the media, the journalists sent to cover him, pushed together in the middle of the crowd, housed in a little pen made of bike racks.

I showed up at the bar dressed as a Trump reporter, complete with a notebook and my actual TRUMP Make America Great Again press pass from a recent rally in Dallas. To this I had added bandages around my head and a fake black eye. Happy Halloween, I thought, stupidly. I didn't yet appreciate that while Trump could be mean he might also be scary and dangerous.

That realization landed a little more than a month later, when I was at a rally inside the belly of a battleship (turned museum) off the coast of South Carolina. Trump had just announced that he wanted to ban all Muslims from entering the United States "until our country's representatives can figure out what the hell is going on" and the mood at the rally was dark. The air around me felt somehow flammable, like the air around a gas station. I was afraid that Trump himself would strike the match. And of course he did.

"She's back there, little Katy. She's back there," he said. "Third rate reporter, remember that, third rate. Third rate."

Afterward a Trump staffer stopped me and said, "These guys are going to walk you out." I looked over and saw two Secret Service agents who guided my producer and me along the gangway and back to our car. It was pitch black and I was worried. We were parked with the crowd.

The question I kept getting asked after that was why didn't you quit? I could have asked for another assignment. I could have bowed out on the grounds of safety. I could have moved back to London. I still had my flat. But then again, why would I run? Sometimes my mother would watch the coverage and call me up aghast. "My God, he sounds so much like your father." Other times, old family friends who had known or worked with my father would email me, especially after seeing Trump directly address, or attack, me from the stage. "Trump has no idea who he's dealing with," they'd say.

They meant it as a compliment. As in Trump had no idea who I grew up with.

My father would call too from time to time.

"These people are crazy," she'd say. "Watch your back."

I didn't need the reminder. My parents faced angry calls and letters and even death threats. After my father testified in the Denny trial, the police came by for wellness checks. My father carried a gun and taught us to live in fear of intruders. I think that some part of me believed that journalism just came with that level of risk.

On a subconscious level I think it felt right.

One night, in January 2016, on a rare day back in New York, Tony and I were out at a falafel place not far from his apartment in Park Slope. I was tired of hotels and desperate for a feeling of home, even if it meant his divorced dad special, a very small and very run-down studio apartment. The first time I visited, he opened the door and stamped his feet around before letting me in.

"To scare off the goats," he said.

He meant cockroaches.

I didn't care.

Things were great with us. Maybe a little roach problem would have put off other people, maybe there was a time when it would have put off me, but I just wanted to be with him. It turned out there was something comforting, especially in New York, about dating a guy who had kids. He could be trusted. He was an adult. He didn't play the games. He was responsible. He was clear and direct. It was refreshing. For the first time in my life, everything in the relationship was just easy.

Except for the travel.

I was always gone and it left our relationship in a low gear, grinding on with slower progress than I think either of us wanted. But I had an idea. Or we had an idea. And it started in that little falafel place, where Tony read about a wild story unfolding in Oregon. An armed group of men were staging an occupation of federal land. Tony had written about the movement and issues behind it when he was at the old *Newsweek*. He knew the story and all the players.

He was also at a professional crossroads. His dream had always been magazines, a dream he'd sort of accomplished when he was named a staff writer for *Newsweek* in 2007. The magazine at the time was owned by the Washington Post Company, edited by a Pulitzer-winner in Jon Meacham, and enjoying the afterglow of yet another National Magazine Award, amid yet another profitable year.

Newsweek in 2007 was still *Newsweek*, in other words: read by millions, staffed by titans, and full of the twentieth-century charm of the print industry. Tony still talks about all of it, a lot, with a whole lot of detail. The free dinners and booze every Friday night in a wood-paneled dining room. The annual retreat to Jamaica. The black cars to anywhere, even for the interns.

All that collapsed before his eyes, with him still inside the building, crawling out with the rest of the younger writers, looking for a new start. After the book, he joined NBC as a writer in a new "Enterprise Unit," a digital-hybrid thing that was eliminated in a couple of years. He turned to short videos for MSNBC and NBC because, well, it seemed like it paid better and he needed the money. He was also realizing something else: he loved it even more than print work.

Our falafel shop plan was to get him into the big time, or at least the bigger time, when it came to television. I told him, if he wanted to be on TV—move to a platform that would still allow him to be a journalist but had some stability and a better paycheck—he should write a note and pitch himself onto the Oregon land story.

"Now?" he asked.

"Now," I said. "Tell them you can get on a plane immediately." He did and he did.

On his third or fourth day in Oregon, he landed a bonkers live interview with a man who had dragged a rocking chair to the end of the main access road. He was sitting in the cold and dark with a shotgun over his lap and a blue tarp over his head to protect him from the snow. He was one of the occupiers, staying up all night to meet the FBI if they cared to arrest him. Tony calmly asked the man how far he was willing to take this fight and the man promised not to turn himself in peacefully. A few weeks later, he made good on that promise. He was shot to death by the FBI.

After that, MSNBC sent Tony on more stories, and when the presidential primaries began he had a surprise for me. It was February 2016 and I was in New Hampshire, the second state to vote, feeling lonely when my phone rang.

"Guess where I am?" he said.

"Where?"

"Getting on a plane for Manchester, New Hampshire."

"What!"

"They put me on the campaign trail."

Our relationship was still somewhat secret, though I guess the MSNBC senior team might have noticed us sneaking off together. We'd meet downstairs in 30 Rock, then sneak up a back stairwell, into a more corporate, non-news wing of the building and make out like the kids we were.

The trail was extraordinary, and exhausting, and exhilarating, and it left little time to overthink things. No time to get worked up about the small things that had sometimes plagued my other relationships. Every day was a new plane. Every day was a new event. Tony was now on the road almost as much as I was, landing a few days ahead of every primary vote to talk with voters. While I covered Trump, he covered the people who might vote for him.

It didn't always mean we were in the same city, but often Tony would fly or drive hours out of his way to join me for a night, sharing road food and scratchy hotel sheets. It was how we really fell in love. A cross-country Fred and Ginger tango to the tune of the American presidential election.

———

In May we were both in Louisville covering Trump's address to the NRA. I was inside navigating my way through supporters who enjoyed heckling me, and Tony was outside interviewing the crowds that had lined up but couldn't get into the packed event. Later that night he woke me up in a panic. "I don't think I can have any more kids," he said. The room we were in had two single beds and we were jammed up together in one. He told me he'd been wrestling with it and the answer was no.

I got out of bed. In shock, but calm. This was the deal-breaker. The nonnegotiable.

"I guess we'll break up then," I said.

"I guess so," said Tony.

I moved to the other bed.

I got up the next morning cool and collected but also still in shock. I called my mom, who loved Tony. She had heard him on *Fresh Air*, way back in 2015, when I was still in London, dating Benoit, and she had called me up to say that she had the perfect man for me. At the time I just rolled my eyes. I knew she wasn't thrilled about my getting serious with a Frenchman. She worried it would mean I was never coming home. My first move to New York she could handle. But living overseas forever was too much. What would happen when I had kids, her grandkids? How would she ever have a meaningful relationship with them? It was so unclear to her that she started pushing random guys she heard on the radio. Anything to get me home.

"He has a crazy father just like you!" she said.

I had no recollection of this conversation until I revealed to her that I was dating a guy named Tony.

"See, mothers do know best!" she said.

What do you mean? I wondered.

"That's the guy I told you to date! Don't you remember? I heard him on *Fresh Air*!"

I laughed. I still did not remember.

But that was then. When I relayed what Tony was now saying about not wanting more kids, her grandkids, her response was immediate.

"Cut him loose," she said. "Nonnegotiable."

Tony and I went the whole day without talking to each other. No texts, no phone calls. I felt deflated. I couldn't eat anything. But I tried not to think about it. I had a *Nightly News* package to write and a thousand MSNBC hits.

After my live shot on *Nightly*, Tony texted asking me to meet him inside the convention showroom where all the guns were on sale. Five hundred thousand square feet of firearms! "Freedom's largest celebration," bragged the NRA's website.

Tony was sitting on a bench in front of a grenade launcher. No really, a grenade launcher. I wondered if he picked the location to send me some sort of message. It was pretty bang on the nose. Were we really going to pull the pin on this relationship or get in the foxhole together?

"I think I'm being stupid," he said. "I don't want to lose you."

"I don't want to lose you, either, but I can't be with you if kids are off the table. I want kids. My mom agrees."

"Your mom loves me," he said.

"She does. But not more than she wants grandkids."

We sat together and talked some more as a troop of Boy Scouts came over to play with the grenade launcher.

"It will be fine. We'll figure it out together," he said.

Tony was stressed about his job on the road and how he was supposed to handle the travel and his kids' big visit in the summer.

He was also stressed about work. He'd been on television regularly for months, but MSNBC hadn't yet offered him a job and no one else had come calling either. He was panicking.

Then the weather warmed, and I gave him some advice.

He was down in Arizona. A hot and dusty Old West kind of location near the border. A scene for music videos and westerns as much as a news report. He called me to ask what he should wear for the shoot he was on. I told him to put his button-downs away.

"Wear one of your black T-shirts," I said.

He objected.

"Just do it," I said.

He agreed but I wasn't finished yet.

"And do some push-ups before you go on," I said. "Do a hundred push-ups."

He groaned.

I was sort of joking. Sort of not. He was an all-state baseball player, college scholarship, Division 1, captain of his team, but he didn't like people assuming he was a jock. And he didn't want to give up his magazine uniform of chunky glasses and professorial coats that he'd been wearing for nearly a decade.

He relented.

And surprise, surprise: ABC called that very week.

Maybe they were planning on calling anyway. Maybe it was just the content of what he was saying. Maybe his agent was actually earning her commission. Or maybe it was the push-ups. I don't know.

But then MSNBC suddenly realized he was worth locking down too, so they made an offer.

That gave him the opening he needed to walk both offers down to CBS, the network with the richest tradition in writing—and pitch himself.

He was hired.

He also negotiated a month of gap time in the summer to be with his kids.

I was thrilled for him.

But just before they arrived, something happened that made Tony doubt I was *the one*, though I wouldn't find out about it until years later over lamb vindaloo and too much tequila.

I had moved my things into Tony's roach motel sometime in January. It was a crazy timetable, I know. We'd been together less than six months. But it wasn't as if I was really moving in. Most of my belongings were still in London. I wasn't going to join the lease. I just didn't want to go back to a hotel and I needed a place to stuff my extra clothes in between campaign trips.

"It's just a few bags," I said, "and I'll only be there a few days a month."

On one of the rare days when we were both home, I got a call from a friend of my father's. I don't remember who it was or how they got my number. I picked it up because I thought it might be a source or even possibly Trump himself. He'd called before from blocked or unrecognizable numbers. I wasn't letting anything go to voicemail.

"Hello," I said.

"Katy?"

"Yes."

"I'm a friend of your father's."

I seized up as they continued. They explained that my father was struggling. There had been an incident, some sort of argument, and Zoey had exploded in anger. This person knew what tended to follow the anger and they were worried.

"I think she's depressed and I think you need to call her," they said. "I don't know what she might do and I'm afraid for her. But I can't take care of her anymore. You have to step in and watch out for her."

I burst into tears. Tony sat up in bed and tried to figure out what was happening with me, but I pushed him away. We still hadn't talked much about our families and this wasn't a moment to start.

"I can't do this," I said. "I can't do this."

I had fifteen thousand unread emails, hundreds of unread texts, a flight first thing in the morning, and the day after that and the day after that for who knows how long. I had slept in my own bed for no more than eight nights since June of 2015. I was living out of a pair of suitcases. And I had a presidential candidate inspiring death threats against me. I could only deal with one crazy at a time. I wouldn't survive two. It was like my mom leaving all over again. I fled Los Angeles so I wouldn't drown alongside my dad and now I was being asked to come back and start swallowing water.

I hung up and called my brother.

"Do you think she will hurt herself?"

"No," he said.

"Are you sure? How do you know?"

"I just know. It'll be fine. Don't worry."

I worried.

This was Tony's first real introduction to my family beyond the stuff he read about online, an introduction so rocky he thought for a moment his girlfriend might be unstable. That maybe this explained why a successful woman was in a relationship with him at all. A guy with no money, living in a cockroach-infested hole-in-the-wall, who had a career in transition and two young children.

It looked like a big red flag but he just waved it off. He didn't have time to worry about it and, besides, I would be on another plane in the morning.

So he trusted me.

And I began to trust us.

––––––

My brother was right about Zoey.

Not long after that call, she walked into a diner wearing a black cowboy hat and pink tank top that read "UNFUCK THE WORLD." She ordered chili, which she spoon-fed to Leica, her little terrier, and she talked and talked and talked—launching into another public airing of our personal issues along with a dizzying tale of the legend of Bob Tur as she saw it, this time with a writer from *The Hollywood Reporter.*

The magazine met my father by her home in Los Angeles because of a hit (and ultimately Oscar-winning) documentary called *O.J.: Made in America.* It's not my father's film, but she stars in it as herself, delivering a mesmerizing series of interviews on Los Angeles, O.J., and the state of America. She does it all from the perspective of a self-described "recovering white male," and I have to admit she's good in the doc. She's also good copy for this magazine reporter. She somehow managed to anticipate what would be one of the major conversations of 2021 and 2022. Is America headed for a new era of political violence?

We were in a fragile truce, she claimed, and Donald Trump had come along to break it for his own benefit.

––––––

For the entire campaign, I tried to cover what in many cases could not be covered, not in the sense of knowing what motivates Trump, what drives his angers and unexpected alliances. His personal interests were so complicated as to almost defy mapping. It was hard to say where his goals ended and the nation's began. I spent 510 days on the Trump campaign, and I was proud of the work, confident that we did our best as an industry. But on election night, I felt sick with worry—estranged from my father and frustrated by the limits of my profession. I wasn't lost, not yet, but I was on my way.

CHAPTER TEN

"Now the Fun Begins"

"Oh, hey, come over here," said Tony.

He looked up at the ceiling and took a deep breath. It seemed like he was trying to drain tears back into his head. Then he looked back at me. It was a long, unblinking stare. The kind of focused attention he gives when he's exceptionally nervous. The intensity made me feel suddenly bashful.

We had a reservation to get to, a good one at a restaurant by our house—a pseudo-secret place that you have to enter through another restaurant. But I'd had a feeling I'd want to look a little nicer than normal on this otherwise normal Saturday night in January. It was cold, so I had to be strategic. I put on a tight black dress that's also a turtleneck, a pair of black stockings, and black suede knee-high boots. Chic but warm. And subtle enough to not outshine anything else I might end up wearing by night's end.

"I can't find something, can you come help me?" he said.

Oh my God.

I found him in the corner of our apartment, rummaging around in the couch for some reason. We'd been in that apartment a month or so, but between the Trump inauguration and Tony's work at CBS, we still had almost no furniture. The rug only covered a fifth of the living room floor, the sofa only a third of that. We had no dining room table, no chairs, no shelves, no television. The bed was on the floor. But here was this beautiful man, currently searching for something in the couch.

Tony had wanted to go to a hotel for the weekend, the Standard in the East Village, the place I had been living in, out of a suitcase, when we'd first met. He'd wanted to make it a surprise but he couldn't stop himself from telling me about it the week before. The same way he sent me pictures of rings just to be sure. He can't keep a secret. Even when he tried, I could still figure out what was going on. He's been on the phone with the hotel all week.

Can you make sure we get that room?

Are there barbecue chips?

How late do you do room service?

He thought he was keeping the calls hush-hush but noise travels when you have no furniture. I didn't care. I loved that I never had to guess what was coming with Tony. I was just excited for the weekend. But as we got closer to Friday, I didn't want to go anywhere. I wanted the surprise but I didn't want to pack a bag for it. I'd been packing and unpacking for so long, from the campaign to the inauguration, I needed to stop moving. I needed to be rooted to a spot, especially if what I assumed was about to happen, happened.

But right then Tony didn't look so sure of the new plan. He was futzing with the couch.

Had he just hid something underneath the cushion?

He stood up and put his hands on my arms and rubbed them up and down.

Was he really doing this now? By the sad blue couch, under the fluorescent ceiling lights?

"Katy," he said with a deep long sigh.

Oh my God he's getting on one knee.

"I love you," he said reaching underneath the cushion again.

I knew what was coming and I knew what I was going to say but my heart froze all the same. He finally located and produced a small black velvet box.

I could see him talking but I could no longer hear a word of what he was saying.

It was like sound stood still, alongside time.

Then he opened the box. Inside was a ring. Gold with a single circular diamond.

He took my hand and looked up at me. I could feel his heart beating in his fingers. My breath caught in my lungs. I knew what I was about to say. I'd known since our fifth date. But doubts raced through my mind as well, doubts about everything that will change if I say "yes."

I saw my flat in London again, then Paris, then my passport, British Airways, an Indian restaurant in Surabaya, a traffic jam in Jakarta, the Venice canals, a plate of squid ink pasta, crooked houses in Amsterdam, the funicular in Budapest.

You can't just move back, I thought. It will be two of you now. Two people. Two lives. Two careers. Two decision makers. No more independent Katy. This means forever. He'll be here, every day, every night. All the time. You sure?

I dodged them like slow-motion bullets in *The Matrix*.

But when I opened my mouth to answer, Tony stood up.

"No no no. Stop, don't answer. That was all wrong. I messed it all up, let me do it again."

I laughed. He was acting like this proposal was something he could shoot and edit later. Like he could rerack the tape, say 3-2-1, and then read it again.

He got back down on his knee and said something about a simple honest proposal for a simple honest love. My heart was so thunderous, it sounded like it was beating in my ears. Once again, I didn't hear a thing he was saying. Until the question. This time I heard it, loud and clear, no doubts, no questions, no flashes of Paris or pasta.

"Will you marry me?"

Yes! I tried to scream it but it came out in a squeak. I was crying and hugging him.

"Want to put on the ring?" he asked, laughing.

"Yes! But first can you do it one more time?"

"Propose?"

"Yes, with the speech. I want to remember it."

He did.

After, we went to dinner and made it official with an announcement in the newspaper, aka Instagram. Me, Tony, cocktail glasses, and a ring.

Caption: Breaking News.

Donald Trump was going to the White House and I was not.

This was strange to a lot of people.

Every election cycle, at every network and every newspaper and every magazine and every website, writers and correspondents vie to be assigned to the strongest candidate. The idea is, you start the beat early, make contacts, learn lots, and arrive in Washington like a veteran. This is why the head of newsgathering had joked with me back in 2015 when I got the assignment that if Trump wins, I'd go to the White House.

No one had expected him to win. Even on election day, there was a widespread assumption that Hillary Clinton would win. That meant the White House team would be the people who covered her plus maybe another veteran correspondent. It would not be the new girl from London.

But when Trump flipped the White House, he flipped the White House beat along with it. His win put the Trump campaign reporters, including myself, on more of an inside track. Still, the network never offered me a White House job and I never asked for it.

"Sending you to Washington would start NBC off on a war footing," I was told, not by NBC but by one of the incoming White House's most senior officials. He was referring to my coverage. I remember thinking, wow, if Trump thinks I'm tough, wait until he faces the White House press corps.

I didn't care to push the issue.

I admit the White House had been a dream of mine since my first days in news way back at my first job when I was an assistant to the news director at KTLA. For an hour each day I'd steal away from my responsibilities—of getting coffee, making copies, opening mail, answering calls—to watch the White House press briefing. I'd give it my full attention. Turn off the phone. Minimize my email. Turn up the dial on the tiny television on my desk. Then with MSNBC on, I'd imagine I wasn't a twenty-two-year-old news assistant but a member of the White House press corps, pen in the air, competing for the floor with David Gregory and Helen Thomas.

But life comes at you fast and it turns out I was even happier with a little distance.

At the end of the campaign, I cashed in a bazillion frequent-flyer miles, coordinated with some old friends from high school, and flew to Thailand and Vietnam. While Donald J. Trump's transition team was planning his inauguration as the forty-fifth president of the United States, I was in one of the few places where no one would be talking about him. No one would come up to me on the street and ask me how I survived. Or how they would survive. Or how America would survive. No one would even know who I was.

For New Year's Eve, my friends and I went to a bizarrely Havana-themed bar, down an alley in Bangkok. I grabbed a pair of glittery green plastic 2017 glasses—the kind of novelty specs they sell in Times Square before the ball drops—and put them on.

"Thirty seconds until midnight!"

The music got louder. Our bodies sweatier. Someone was passing around cigars. Was that smoke in the air or was the wall getting hazier? My eyes couldn't focus. My arms and legs were swinging. I was feeling the music or else I was beyond the point of knowing whether I could feel the music. I pointed my phone backwards toward the group of us and pressed record. I wanted to save this moment, so I could get back here later—call it up when I need to be reminded of the way I felt that night.

Which was . . . excited.

I had Tony. Tony was in New York. Choosing life over career, for the first time, felt good. It felt right. My motto used to be, "why be happy when you can be great." Now it felt like why not try being both. Great *and* happy.

Worth a shot, anyway.

———

It was Shep Smith, of all people, who first told me I was getting an anchor job. We were at a Mexican restaurant in Hell's Kitchen. I was gorging myself on guacamole and margaritas when he spotted me and walked over.

"Congratulations on the new gig," he said, clearly a little pleased that he had this bit of industry gossip before anyone else did.

"What gig?" I said.

"You're getting the two p.m. hour."

"I am? No one's told me."

"Your agent didn't tell you? Maybe you should get a new agent."

Two weeks later it turned out Shep was right about the job. I was thrilled. By anchoring my own show, I figured, I'd have the equivalent of a single daily live shot instead of a dozen different live shots. And instead of being limited to a few minutes per hit, I'd be able to sprawl over a full hour, touching whatever topic I like, for whatever amount of time it needed. That was my theory anyway.

I went to Washington to cover the inauguration, my last hurrah as a Trump campaign field reporter. It was hard to find the right tone for the coverage. All of us were struggling, all over the industry. We were dealing with such an imponderable split screen. On one side, you had an incoming American president, the pick of the electoral college, if not the majority of voters, and there was the usual amount of pomp and ceremony on such an occasion.

On the other side, you had the fact that Donald Trump was Russia's pick for president and Vladimir Putin had personally directed a campaign to help him win. Those were the conclusions of our CIA. And our FBI. They had drawn this conclusion with "high confidence," according to a declassified briefing out that very month. And when we delicately said things like, Trump is "dogged by questions about Russia" or "there's a cloud over his election," this is what we were talking about.

It was an astounding fact.

It was also a very hard fact to cover on Inauguration Day, which is a bit like a wedding. For journalists like me, with serious questions, the time to air them was yesterday or tomorrow. Inauguration Day was about hoping for the best.

"Now the fun begins," the president said after his swearing in. "Now the fun begins."

"Mary Tyler Moore died! We just got it confirmed. We're looking for guests. You might have to tap-dance for a bit."

The voice in my ear was my executive producer, a veteran of the business, now working a show with a newbie for an anchor. This was my third week in the chair, and we'd carefully mapped out the show as always, but the death of a Hollywood icon had just cleared the decks. "Tap-dance" meant talk about Mary Tyler Moore off the cuff for as long as it takes to find a guest to join me.

I'd been in a situation like this as the guest, the reporter rushed in to knowingly discuss something that was only barely known publicly. But when you're a reporter, you have a very clear mission. You talk to your sources. You learn things. You tell people what you've learned. That's pretty much it. Once you have a little news judgment, and a little style, you're golden. And after ten years in the business, I was golden.

I knew how to take a jumble of reporting and give it a point, make it a story, end with a punch or sometimes a fun joke. I knew which live shots needed a snarl and which needed a smile. I knew what to wear in every situation, in every kind of weather, and I knew in an instant. I could pack a bag in the dark. I could make a flight in thirty minutes.

I also knew the subtleties of the job. I could tell when my voice was off or my face was wrong. I could make adjustments mid-report. I knew how to tap-dance. Hell, I knew all the dances. I knew when the moment called for a laugh and when a screwup called for an apology. Plus, I was smooth.

But as an anchor, I was kind of a mess.

What did I know about Mary Tyler Moore? I had watched reruns of her show growing up, obviously. I knew she was a feminist icon. What else. Fuck. I went to commercial.

"Can I get a one sheet?" I asked, trying not to sound as frantic as I felt. I pulled out my phone and searched Moore's entry on IMDb, wary, of course, that you can't trust everything you read there but desperate for a refresher, anything before the red light came back on.

It was my first lesson as an anchor.

I didn't have a beat, anymore.

I had a show.

I didn't have to know something.

I had to know *everything*.

The news business is a "great job" culture, as in, "great job" is all you'll hear until the day they fire you for a *not great job*. So I was committed to figuring out anchoring in a hurry.

Practically speaking, that meant figuring out the teleprompter. I hated it at first. I got worse before I got better.

In the first month or so, I got so bad that we experimented with no scripts at all. I told my team to blank out the prompter. Just give bullet points on paper. I'd ad-lib the rest.

But inevitably there would be a story that maybe I didn't know as well as the others, *ahem, Mary Tyler Moore*. You don't realize how distinctive your own internal voice is until you try to read words drafted by someone else. It's like slipping on someone else's shoe.

Even if it's the same size, it's worn in all different places and you stumble when you walk.

That was me on camera in those early days.

Stumble, trip. Stumble, trip. Stumble, trip.

I had to learn how to focus on the words, but also blur them. I had to surrender to the read, but also be present for the meaning. It's the difference between knowing a dance and doing the steps. For a while, I could do it if I wasn't thinking about it. But the problem was, I was always thinking about it. How could I not be thinking about it? I was the one doing it. I couldn't do it and not think about it. But the biggest stumbles often came the moment I realized I wasn't stumbling.

I'd be a minute into a rip-roaring opening to a show, seeing the words, reading the words, investing each one with exactly the meaning I intended. And then *wham*. Suddenly, I'd get an outside perspective on myself, and a new thought would surge, a realization: I'm doing it! No stumbles! Yes! YES!

Then I'd stumble.

Clothes were their own kind of nightmare.

A month into my job, the *Daily Mail* called out an anchor in Australia for wearing the same outfit on two occasions within half a year. (Headline: "That's Thrifty!") There's also an incalculable amount of leering at the news. Some of the women who cover business are written about as "money honeys." There's at least one network where all the women are supposedly required—or at least strongly urged—to wear body-contouring, candy-colored outfits. Every woman in news has heard some version of the phrase: shoulders back, tits up. Sometimes the message is subtler but the intention is unmistakable. Your looks matter. This isn't radio.

In my twenties, I did a dumb dog segment in a tight dress and someone clipped it and put it online. They called out their favorite and least favorite parts of me and dozens of commentators did the same. For years it was one of the first things that came up when you googled my name. To this day my husband tells me there are body-part-related clips of me on YouTube with hundreds of thousands of views.

Well, I wasn't taking any chances.

Have you heard of this new thing called a blazer? Men wear them a lot. Now I do too. Blazer over a blouse. Blazer over a dress. Blazer over a blazer if could. I'm the *SNL* sketch of Suze Orman. I don't get them at Joann's Phoenix Jacket Junction. But I do get them.

I want to look like myself and I want our *coverage* to keep you interested.

———

About that coverage: I knew for sure that I didn't want it to be partisan. I wanted to be fair. The struggle, as we moved into Trump's presidency, was the reality that fair meant we had to note that the president said incorrect things, a lot. More than past presidents. It was daily.

I also knew for sure that my hour should be big-picture and deep. But while viewers always allege that they want in-depth, nonpartisan coverage, the ratings throughout the industry suggest that while that's an appreciation, it's not a passion. It doesn't win the ratings or clicks. Journalism is a public service, but the journalism industry is a business. If you look away, the business fails and the service withers with it.

So it's all a balance. You try to be even-tempered, almost serene. Even when you're covering a tipped Porta-Potty of political news. In that first year, the ratings were up, way up, insanely elevated by the insane stuff coming out of Washington. We're talking double-digit increases over what were already double-digit increases during the

2016 campaign, all across the network. And while every network was up, we were routinely beating CNN for the first time in years. Even in my hour, a time when people might be expected to tune out, take a break, viewership was consistently over a million people.

That's a lot of people.

It had been a bumpy onboarding for Tony as well. The reason Tony wasn't on *Evening News* on most nights, the reason he could so often meet me after my show, was a major screwup shortly after he started.

In August of 2016, just a few weeks into his new job, he'd been told to head over to Trump Tower. There was a guy climbing the building using some sort of suction cup contraption. It was a maybe hilarious, maybe scary situation. No one knew what the guy wanted or what he planned to do. The Republican candidate for president lived and worked on the top floor, so whatever the stakes, they were more than zero.

Tony had no idea. He wasn't that kind of news guy. In fact, if anyone at *Evening News* had read the new hire note that went around, they'd have seen that he had more than a decade of report-ing and writing experience, but most of it in long-form features, not breaking news. Or maybe they did read the note and it was August and Tony was the only person in the building and so he was sent. Either way, disaster loomed.

First, his clothes. This had the potential to become a terrorist situation, but Tony had left the office in clothes that had the po-tential to become a party situation: a lime green button-down and a blue linen coat.

Second, his hair. I had told him to wear it big down in Arizona because it was rugged terrain. This was midtown Manhattan. There were suits and ties in the shops behind him and there were salons on every block. He looked like a sunstruck tourist on a gambol toward the next rooftop bar.

Third, his smile. This was a hard-news story. It was scheduled to run in the first block of the *CBS Evening News* with Scott Pelley. It was not a whimsical tale about a crazy kid who bet his buddies he could climb a building. Maybe it could have been, but that's not how CBS saw it. Not with the streets closed and a special climbing unit of the New York Police Department popping out windows and trying to grab the guy on live television.

Oh, and that wasn't the worst part. They told him he had a minute-long report at 6:40, but right at 6:30 the police were closing in, so the show came to Tony early. He heard the introduction from Pelley, but it was ten minutes before he was scheduled to go on. He was confused. He didn't know what was happening.

Was the show even on? Maybe Pelley was practicing? Maybe it was a tease?

Tony had no idea. But he figured, well, I'd better assume this is real, which was the right call. So, when Pelley finished the introduction, he just started talking and, aside from the big hair and the lime shirt and the stupid smirk, it was going pretty well.

Until he heard a producer yell "No."

Tony stopped cold on live television. He stared over at the producer. His earpiece filled with a dozen other producers yelling at him. Everybody wanted him to start talking again, but he couldn't make out what they were saying. The seconds ticked by. Millions and millions of households wondered what had happened to the *CBS Evening News.* And when Tony looked again at his producer on scene, he suddenly realized she had not said "No" at all.

The word had been "Go."

She was telling him to start and then encouraging him along. And what had he done? He basically laid down on live television.

Evening News didn't ask him back for months.

For Tony, it turned out to be kind of a blessing. He got to pour his time into TV's version of long-form—deep, reported pieces for *Sunday Morning* and what is now *CBS Mornings*, which, no surprise, he now co-anchors.

———

It also worked out well for me. We often got to ride the train home together to Brooklyn. Tony would first walk from CBS to NBC, then we'd head downward and back in time. The NBC studios are brand-new, the building's elevators old, and the lobby even older. 30 Rockefeller Plaza was built in the 1930s and filled with iconic pieces of art. It's all murals and mosaics that trumpet the March of Progress, the triumph of knowledge over ignorance.

Some days I felt like I was living up to the message. But only on some days.

In general, most Americans don't trust our work.

The work of mainstream news organizations.

No journalist under the age of thirty-five, in fact, has ever had a day in their life in which they could honestly say that most Americans generally trusted what they do.

That's what the Gallup polls have been saying for decades.

They've been asking the question since 1972: "In general, how much trust or confidence do you have in the mass media?" They specify newspapers, radio, and television. They define trust in terms of reporting the news fully, accurately, and fairly.

The results are awful.

Awful.

Trust peaked after Watergate in 1974—nearly 70 percent of people had a great deal or at least a fair amount of trust in mainstream media. By the Clinton era, it was down to 53 percent. By the Bush era, down to 44 percent. And during the Trump years, it hit a new low of 32 percent.

If we sold yogurt, and most people didn't trust it, we'd be out of business. If we sold tires, and most people had doubts, we'd go under. But news ratings were soaring. You may roll your eyes because you've heard all this before. You may say it's a result of audiences sorting themselves into different silos, or social media making it next to impossible to reach anyone outside your bubble. But none of that changes the numbers. More people than ever were watching or reading the news. But fewer people than ever were trusting it.

For that whole first year, I struggled to reconcile those two facts and I worried about what they meant for the country. Something had to give.

That concern all came pouring out of me in December of 2017, when I was invited to be a guest on *The Late Show with Stephen Colbert*.

All in all, I'd had maybe the best year of my life.

Besides learning to anchor, I'd also written a book. In August of 2016, Jen Ortiz, an editor at *Marie Claire*, had asked me if I wanted to write a piece about covering Trump, which I did. That resulted in a call from an editor named Julia Cheiffetz, asking me if I wanted to turn it into something more. Every night since election night I'd come home from my day job and write furiously. The book, published in June, was a hit.

Plus, Tony and I got married.

We did it on our own terms. First, we sat down and googled "best resort in America." I'll leave the exact results of that search to your imagination because it will no doubt change over the years, and because the only real answer to such a search is personal. The best hotel in America is whatever hotel you need. In fact, I can make a pretty strong case for any hotel that is actually located inside an airport.

Hello Orlando International Hyatt! Hello extra hour of sleep!

But at that moment, our best hotel in America was in the middle of nature out west. The booking began with us committing to room rates and fees higher than the price of any car either of us has ever owned. It ended with a question, the financial version of being mistaken for French.

Will you be flying private?

No, we'll be flying Delta.

May we arrange a driver?

No, my husband has points with Avis.

And so, we got in a Chevy Malibu and drove from the airport.

Our first stop was a little county clerk's office for what was essentially a drive-up marriage license. We both got a little misty as the lady behind the desk—a lady with perhaps the most consistently pleasant desk job in America—gave us the official paperwork of love.

The hotel, we soon discovered, turned out to be worth every letter of that Google search. We checked in fine and were shown to a room with a view of the elements, of nature, of time itself. But the next morning at breakfast, we got a little lesson in the here and now.

The couple next to us was chatty and handsomely dressed and the woman was looking over at us, scanning for a way to start a conversation. On the surface I knew it'd be about the great food or the wonderful patio. But I also noticed that the diamond ring on her finger was the size of a small strawberry. I sensed that what we'd really be talking about was affluence. And status. And whether we had enough to justify them talking to us for more than a few minutes.

"Isn't the bread just amazing," she said.

Tony nodded with a face full of it.

"So good," I said.

"When did you get here?" she said.

"Just last night."

"Hmmmm," the woman said. "How long are you staying?"

"Just until Sunday," I said.

Tony jumped in.

"We have to get back for work," he said.

"Oh, too baaaaad," the woman said. "Have you slept under the stars yet? We did it last night. The sky bed was amazing."

Sky bed? We had no idea what she was talking about.

A thought fell on the table like bird poop and we all saw it. Some of the rooms have sky beds. Some do not. Ours is of the latter quality. Ever so casually, the woman turned her diamond toward her palm, hiding it from us as the conversation withered and died.

To be honest, we preferred it that way.

The next day was the day we'd been planning. By not planning. I wore red and Tony wore black. Together we climbed to the top of, what the hotel said was, a 750-million-year-old rock formation to say "I do." Aside from the hotel manager/wedding officiant calling Tony "Tom" a couple of times, it was perfect.

My life was good. Really good. I wanted to focus on it. Savor it. But at the same time, I also knew that while it was maybe the best year of my life, it was only my life and certainly not the best year in the life of the country. That's what made my Colbert appearance so complicated. I knew that the invite was not exactly a sign of good times in dear old America.

CHAPTER ELEVEN

"Thinks She Is Cronkite"

Somehow worse than being hounded by paparazzi is being spotted by paparazzi and judged not worth dropping the cigarette. Or that's what I'm assuming. I've never been hounded. I pulled up to the guest entrance at the Ed Sullivan Theater where *The Late Show* is taped, to the tiny stage door that the paparazzi stake out. But when I stepped out of my car, I stepped out not to camera snaps but to murmurs of "who's this?"

I couldn't blame them, exactly. The person who walked in a few minutes before me was Jodie Foster. She was there to pretape an interview for later in the week. What was I doing following in the literal footsteps of Jodie Foster?

Inside the theater, the air smelled like old New York, like afternoon newspapers, your wife cooking dinner, and cocktails on a tray. It also smelled like television, or the making of television, anyway, like decades of heavy wiring and dust and electricity. The airtight door in front of me led directly to the stage, but the "ON AIR" sign above it was still dark. We were at least an hour before the taping and many hours before the show airs.

"Katy Tur!"

A production assistant with a clipboard greeted me, and told me I'm awesome, and then studied her paperwork to see what "awesome" would get me in terms of a dressing room. A friend had already coached me on what to expect. To the left was a two-room area with a private bathroom. Upstairs was the big one. I was in neither.

The assistant guided me downstairs to an area under the stage, where giant wooden trusses support the ceiling. I learned later the Colbert team calls this area "the pit." Apparently, Ed Sullivan's original team installed the trusses before bringing out a Ringling Brothers elephant act in the mid-fifties. Back then, partisanship in America was so nonexistent that the American Political Science Association issued a plea for more of it: "Alternatives between the parties are defined so badly that it is often difficult to determine what the election has decided even in broadest terms."

My dressing room was lovely, even without a window. There was a spread of fresh bread, cheeses, sweet and salty snacks, and a fridge that I opened with excitement. Packages of "birthday cake" flavored truffle balls fell out. I was about to open one when someone knocked at the door. I looked to the NBC PR person who was with me that night. She shrugged. I shrugged back and opened it.

A different production assistant had a question.

"Tom Hanks would like to stop by to say hello. Is that okay?"

No, please tell the nicest guy in Hollywood to fuck off, I thought sarcastically.

"Yes, that'll be fine."

Tom Hanks likes journalists, or at least he values independent journalism.

In the nineties, he noticed that the coffee machine in the Clinton White House briefing room was an old filter thing. Plastic. Half melted. I picture it molded over after the last pour before a holiday break. Hanks replaced it with a fancy espresso machine.

In 2004, he did it again for the journalists covering the Bush White House. Then he replaced that machine in 2010 for everyone covering Barack Obama. And again in 2017. This time for the press covering Donald Trump. Someone put his note on the wall with yellow tacks and someone else put it on social media, where everyone ran with it like a commentary on Donald Trump, which to be fair it might have been.

"Keep up the good fight for Truth, Justice, and the American Way," the note read. "Especially the Truth part."

When he appeared in the doorway, he was in all gray tone: gray shirt, darker gray pants, slightly graying hair. At first, I just stared. I stared for the same reason everyone stared, as though I wasn't sure if he really existed in three-dimensional form until that very moment. I expected him to slide under the door as a series of pixels. Maybe an assistant would roll in an old television and say, now a message from the actor Tom Hanks (presses play).

Tom Hanks, the real live person and not a recording, told me he was a big fan of my work on the campaign trail.

You did a good job, he said. Hell of a campaign.

I was in shock, so I barely said anything, but I did give him one of my books.

He was on the show to talk about *The Post*, a new movie about the clattering heroism of old-school journalism. I hadn't seen the movie yet, but we've all seen a version of it. Smoke-filled rooms. Terrible comb-overs. Scant female journalists. The glory of the pen (and the penis, basically), as fresh bundles of newspaper land like bombs all over Washington.

Hanks was playing star editor Ben Bradlee. "He was like a model of a newsman" is how Stephen Colbert described the character. And Tom Hanks agreed. "Oh, he lived and died for it," he said.

I watched their interview on a giant television in my dressing room. Hanks was encouraged into doing his Ben Bradlee impression, which was deliciously good. It came out as a whiskey- and tobacco-cured growl. "If you're gonna put it on the front page," he said, with a dramatic pause, "it better be right," dramatic pause, "because if it's wrong, you got to eat it," extra dramatic pause, "and it doesn't taste good."

The crowd loved it.

I did too until I started thinking about it a little more. Hanks's performance was excellent, but this golden gods of journalism act isn't fair.

Colbert squared up a clip from the movie. In the clip, a half dozen or so *Washington Post* reporters are standing around a box. In the box is the Pentagon Papers, a top secret report about the Vietnam War, protected by a court order. If the paper publishes anything from it, they could all be accused of treason and jailed. Plus, they have only ten hours until deadline. The group is panicked.

"How are we supposed to comb through four thousand pages," someone says. "There's no way we can possibly do this."

Ben Bradlee is undeterred.

He picks up a chunk of the report and says, in that growl we just heard from the Hanks on Colbert's couch: "Thanks to the president of the United States, who by the way, is taking a shit all over the First Amendment, we have the goods." He puts his feet up on a desk. "So we dig in." End clip.

Stories like these cast a long cold shadow over our own. They foster the idea that these great icons of the past built an industry, then my generation came along and broke it all. But guess what? If

Ben Bradlee put that assessment on his front page, he'd have to eat it. Because it'd be wrong.

And it wouldn't taste good.

If you've been a broadcast journalist for any amount of time, you've had the experience of being compared to Walter Cronkite and chances are the comparison was not a favorable one. I've actually won a Walter Cronkite Award for Excellence in Television Political Journalism, and accepting the award at the National Press Club in Washington, D.C., might be one of the proudest moments of my career. The citation said my work on the 2016 campaign deserved to be celebrated for "demonstrating the honor of [my] profession."

Except, according to every critic with a smartphone, the opposite is true. "Cronkite would be turning over in grave [*sic*] if he saw Katy Tur," reads a typical, typo-prone message I get almost daily. "Thinks she is Cronkite," chides another. "Katy Tur is a turd," remarks a third. "These young journalists need to take time and sit down and watch the great TV journalists of the past. Cronkite comes to mind."

There are only so many times you can be told to be more like Cronkite before you start wondering aloud to your husband if you really are a fraud (or a tur-d), and then your husband drags you down a rabbit hole to find out more about the God-man from Missouri. So, imagine me now as my husband and I crack open the authorized biography of Cronkite, the man held aloft as the beacon of all that is and ever was good in journalism, written by historian Douglas Brinkley, and I start to read.

We are genuinely excited to delve into the life of "the most trusted man in America." But right away the legend looks a little one-dimensional. Brinkley says that "most trusted man in America" survey was designed to rank politicians not journalists. Cronkite's name appeared alongside Richard Nixon and Ted Kennedy; NBC and ABC News competitors weren't even on the ballot.

So maybe not a great hook to hang your slogan on. But it's just marketing language. A little puffery is okay, right? I could probably learn something about the art of self-promotion. Let's see what else Brinkley found. Oh, here's something interesting. In 1952 Walter Cronkite covered the Republican National Convention, one of the first conventions to be televised. That's got to be chock-a-block with best practices, right?

Actually, Brinkley says that Cronkite conspired to bug a committee room at the convention, then reported what he'd learned on live television. To pull it off, Cronkite had a CBS technician run a wire up the side of the hotel and into a broom closet. One of his producers then listened in, running him info for air. That doesn't sound like journalism. That sounds like spying. It also feels a little, I don't know, against the law. But hey, let's give Cronkite a break. He was still finding his footing. TV was new. Mistakes were made.

Let's read ahead to Cronkite's glory years in the sixties and seventies. By then "Uncle Walter" was one of the most famous and affluent men in America. He and his wife and kids would travel around with the families of other famous men, including the novelist James Michener and the *Washington Post* columnist Art Buchwald, Brinkley wrote. The group would go island hopping in the South Pacific, snorkeling, and sailing. They'd play Frisbee.

Sounds great!

But Brinkley reports that Cronkite had struck a deal with Pan Am, one of the largest companies in America at the time. He was getting the trips for free. In other words, he was making at least twenty-five times the typical American family, but he decided to accept a gift of travel from a giant American company he was also liable to be covering. That is definitely the kind of thing that would get me fired today.

Can you imagine? Picture my pasty, pudgy, New York winter of a body crashing into the waves of Fiji or the Cook Islands. When the scandal broke, because it would definitely break, photos would break too. I try to picture Cronkite stumble-walking out of the ocean under a headline in the *Daily Mail* or *New York Post* declaring him a moral catastrophe. That's a link that'll live forever. And this is a career goal? No, no, no.

But, hey, let's look at his work. When people tell me I should learn from the great Walter Cronkite, they're really talking about his journalism. Brinkley reports that former president Lyndon Johnson, near the end of his life, invited Cronkite to his ranch for a final interview. That says something. I can't think of a president who would do that for me. Surely there are some lessons here in the art of the question.

But according to Brinkley, Cronkite and his producing team at CBS faked some of the footage. They shot the interview, then reshot some of the anchor's questions and spliced in the footage to alter the meaning of different moments. For example, Brinkley writes, when LBJ was discussing the Vietnam War—which the public had soured on—Cronkite and company inserted a fake cutaway shot of the great anchor raising a skeptical eyebrow.

I have to say, this is definitely a lose-your-job and never-work-again level offense. Johnson called the edits a game of "dirty pool," and it's only thanks to LBJ's former lawyer—who appears to have been tipped off—that this Frankenstein never aired.

Now maybe you think I'm cherry-picking out of an eight-hundred-page book about a forty-year career, and that's true to some extent. But these are not minor incidents. They're epic failures, and what's remarkable about them today is the extent to which they have either been forgotten or misremembered by the general public. And we haven't even gotten to some of Cronkite's everyday coverage as managing editor of the *CBS Evening News.*

It's hailed today as the kind of bulletproof journalism that defies partisanship.

And yet.

That's not how it played at the time. Brinkley says that Cronkite covered the civil rights movement in such a way that some of the southern CBS affiliates complained and took to calling CBS the "Colored Broadcasting Station." It reminds me of Trump referring to MSNBC as MS-DNC—because he thinks we're too sympathetic to the Democrats. People today are liable to blame us for that accusation and point us back to Cronkite. Well, here I am looking to Cronkite and seeing that he faced the same sort of thing.

Likewise, Cronkite was embraced by people who—if they were active today—we'd call partisans and progressives. I'm talking about leaders of the civil rights movement like Julian Bond, who called Cronkite an "ally." I'm talking about activists opposed to the war in Vietnam, after Cronkite declared it a "stalemate." Daniel Ellsberg, the man who leaked the Pentagon Papers, was so fond of Cronkite that he gave him an exclusive interview *while he was on the run from the FBI.* Cronkite asked softballs, Brinkley reports, and no news came of the conversation except that it happened.

The fact is that Cronkite was "a man of the left," as Brinkley later put it in a C-SPAN interview. He called the Chicago police "a bunch of thugs," wondered why more Americans weren't livid about the My Lai Massacre, implied that Barry Goldwater was some sort of neo-Nazi, and dedicated nearly two thirds of the *Evening News* to Watergate coverage—just days before the 1972 election.

He also urged Robert Kennedy to run for president and was *himself* seriously floated as a running mate for George McGovern.

In return, a lot of conservatives hated him. They wore lapel buttons that said "Stop Cronkite." Others flipped him the finger in public. But this is the man whom journalists today are supposed to emulate if they want to be fair?

Now, look, I understand it was a different time and the standards have changed. But I'm not talking about Brinkley writing about how Cronkite was once spotted in a topless bar, or dining with a go-go dancer not his wife, or narrating a propaganda film for the Pentagon.

I'm talking about his work. Today these failures would be covered, collected, and never forgotten. Cronkite would be hounded daily, his image damaged, and his viewership fractured into the camps we all have to deal with.

Tony and I went back and forth on this a lot because, well, despite my best efforts, critics on Twitter can really drive me crazy. We decided that some of the "greatest" journalists of all time are in fact just the luckiest. Only their best is remembered, but a lot of their work would now be considered the worst of the worst. Journalism today is not a fallen profession and it isn't a perfected one, either. But it's getting better. We still write a rough draft of history, only now it's a more scrupulous and accountable one than ever before because we have nowhere to hide. Everything we do is recorded. And everything we do can be compiled in an instant, used as a hit piece against us. We have to be better, we have no choice.

For the record, I am still very proud to have won a Cronkite award. I still think he is a great journalist. My point is that he was a human being too. He was trying his best just like the rest of us.

———

I have no idea what I'll be remembered for, or by whom, but this is how Stephen Colbert introduces me after Tom Hanks leaves the stage and they swap in a fresh mug, filled with water, for me:

"The president of these United States has called my next guest everything from not a very good reporter to a great reporter, sometimes. Please welcome Katy Tur!"

I'm ostensibly there to promote my book, *Unbelievable*, but at this point—three months after publication, at least six months after writing it—I can barely remember what's in it, and Colbert didn't book me to talk about 2016. He wants to know what the hell is happening now. But it's been a dropped-cafeteria-tray-of-a-year. The result is a mess. I can't easily tell you what it used to be.

Sloppy Joes? Tater Tots? Orange juice?

I tried to refresh my memory before coming on. I checked the Trump timelines, the explainers, the recaps and write-throughs. I perused the morning newsletters and evening newsletters and must-read Twitter accounts and all the usual newspapers and columnists. But the year is not one year but three, not twelve months but thirty-six, and not a year in America as we knew it—but somewhere we did not know. Somewhere new and different.

It's led by a president who attempted to ban immigration from seven Muslim countries.

A president who alleged that he only lost the popular vote because of millions and millions of illegal votes for his opponent.

A president who accused his predecessor of wiretapping his phones.

A president whose campaign is under investigation for conspiring with Russia.

A president not only beloved by many white people but by many white supremacists, whose rise to power drew some comparisons to Hitler.

A president who watched neo-Nazis march in Charlottesville and saw "very fine people on both sides."

This is not normal, not even close, but the truly momentous stuff of the past year can be hard to pick out from the merely dramatic. I admit it's a fine line to draw. But we have to draw it. We can't keep this up. That's how I feel a year into my show and that's what I said—unguardedly and unwisely, no doubt—to a producer from the Colbert show. He just wanted a few tidbits to tell Stephen and maybe one funny anecdote. Instead he got my hot take on how all journalists need to calm the eff down.

Now Stephen is asking me about it.

"You said that everyone covering Trump needs to tone it the— rhymes with duck—down," Colbert says. "What do you mean by that?"

Let's see how this goes.

"I just think that if you take on everything, if you're screaming about everything, if everything is the end of the world . . ."

I'm going to get hammered for appearing to minimize things.

". . . and yes a lot of it is very, very serious, I'm not trying to di- minish what's going on with the Russia investigation, with the norms he's shattering, with the allegations of sexual misconduct, with pos- sible nuclear war with North Korea, thanks for reminding me . . ."

Okay, let's get back to my main point.

". . . I think those are very serious things, but we need to pick and choose what we get breathless about because if you get breath- less about everything, even just a ridiculous tweet, people are not going to take you seriously. You give fodder to this idea that the media is all out to get Donald Trump and we're looking for any reason to criticize him. That's a bad idea. I don't think it's healthy. So that's why I say, tone it the eff down."

I think that came out okay.

But Colbert has a look on his face I can't read. He puts a heavy palm down on the desk and starts talking.

"So you're not always out to criticize Donald Trump," he says.

"No," I say. "Not at all."

"So say something nice about him."

The breath catches in my throat.

Say something nice about him?

The crowd starts to cheer. They think he's got me somehow. I think he does too. But hold on a second. Just because you're not out to criticize someone doesn't mean you're out to compliment them. That's not even the right scale for a journalist. My job is to report, highlight, and evaluate the available facts. And that's my way out of this corner. Stick to the facts.

"His ties are very long," I say.

Colbert agrees.

"He's well-endowed in that area."

Eat that, Ben Bradlee.

CHAPTER TWELVE

"She Left? . . . She Left"

"**M**y daughter does not support the LGBTQ community," my father wrote. "She's transphobic and fearful it will hurt her career in these alt-right times. Career before family. In the words of Paddy Chayefsky: she's pure television. I apologize to you all and will continue to fight for my community."

My father wrote that in the summer of 2017 after *The New York Times* sent a reporter out to profile me for the Styles section. I was excited about the piece and my dad told me she was too—said I did a great job covering Trump. We had a good talk and for a moment she started to acknowledge the pain she caused our family. She even touched on the violence. It was brief and it wasn't quite what I needed but I felt like it was a real start. When the article came out, I saw that the reporter had interviewed my father. It seemed good. She said she was working on our relationship. But for some reason, I still can't figure out exactly what, my dad hated the piece. She said it had left her "humiliated" and seemed outraged over the fact it had landed on "Pride Sunday," adding "the optics could not be worse."

My mom had called me up to tell me about his post. I thought she was joking at first. I told Tony to google it. Then read it. And summarize it for me. I was too hurt, too angry. I felt whiplashed by a relationship that had actually warmed up a little. Even still, I had hope for a reconciliation. A year later I thought that my brother Jamie's graduation from medical school in June 2018 could be it.

I rented a car in Brooklyn, my mom flew in to meet us, and we drove down to Rowan University in New Jersey with Fleetwood Mac playing.

Jamie had taken his time easing into adulthood, or at least the adulthood of training and careers. He went to UCSB, like me, then surfed, traveled, and picked up some substitute teaching work at a school nearby. He was always smarter than I was. In high school, he was so far ahead of his classmates in math that he was given a free period for extra study of his choosing. AP Calculus was too easy.

But his reputation for brains always outstripped his actual record, until now. After graduation, he'd be off to residency at UC Davis, training on two tracks, hospital medicine and psychiatry. In many ways, Jamie was living out my father's fantasy of becoming a doctor and I knew the graduation would be a big occasion for Zoey too. Jamie told me Dad was coming. He warned my mother as well, performing the extra work of keeping the family out of an argument on his big day.

I was nervous about the possibility of a face-to-face with my father, but also a little excited. Estrangement is loss. Estrangement is work. You only do it if you have to. You only do it if you don't have a good alternative. I was hopeful there was still goodwill left. The graduation might at last force a family moment for all of us. Jamie was planning to go out to dinner with Dad alone the night before, but on the day itself—me, my husband, my mom, Jamie, my father, all of us—had a chance to, I don't know, actually. Say hello? Hug and make up? Cry and express regret?

Zoey had never met Tony. Surely at the very least she'd want to see him.

On the car ride there, I prepped Tony for what might go down. He didn't really need to be told, of course. He had experience with tense and awkward when it came to his own father and mother. But I felt better walking him through it and he listened. We both knew I was really just prepping myself. My mom also listened, sitting in the backseat. She was not at ease, but calmer than I was because she had more regular contact with Zoey, if only to talk about the video library.

The sun baked us from the moment we stepped out of the car and we had to hurry. We were late, which meant all the chairs under a large shade tree were gone, so we sat in the heat and sweated and squinted. Was my father here? I saw her a few rows ahead. She'd gotten a spot in the shade. Leica was on her lap, occasionally peering over her shoulder at us, but my father never turned. Not once. If she was aware of our presence, she didn't show it.

When Jamie's name was read we cheered like mad, as loudly as we could, so loud it would have been impossible not to hear us. Impossible not to know that we were Jamie's people, just as we could tell which cluster was there for all the previous graduates. It was a crowd of little groups and we were a group plus Zoey. Still, she never looked back.

After the ceremony, the school offered drinks on the lawn and we milled around with the other families and Jamie. I could see my father now, in what I remember as a white dress with a light green sun shawl, almost the same color as my own jacket. I was in a white dress I'd worn to my own high school graduation, feeling pleased that it still fit me. But also, I realized, wishing for that earlier era in my family's life. It wasn't perfect back then, but it beat this.

Jamie left us and went over to say hello to Dad. I watched him walk over, my heart pounding. For whatever reason, they'd always had an easier relationship. Perhaps Jamie could persuade Dad to come back over with him, I thought, not believing that I should be the one to walk over to her, because I wasn't the one who had walked away and launched a multiyear public attack. But this is how distance develops and lasts. It takes two. It always takes two.

"Where's Dad?" I asked, when Jamie came back over.

"She left," he said.

"She left?"

"She left."

"Really?"

"Yes."

"Did you invite her over?"

"No."

"Why?"

"Because she would have come if she wanted to."

That was my brother. Dry. Analytical. Detached from drama.

And that was it? No hello? Not even a head nod? Not even eye contact? I could have run after her. I could have called her phone and said, we're here, come over, say hi, we miss you, come to lunch, meet Tony, this is dumb, let's celebrate, we're trying for a baby.

But I didn't.

She never looked back.

———

I kept moving. Did I mention that I finally got that trip to Italy? The one I'd put off indefinitely to follow the Trump campaign? It was with my American husband not my French boyfriend, though,

176

and we were on our long-delayed honeymoon. Two whole weeks. Two whole weeks where I could put down my phone and replace it with one Aperol Spritz after another. Much like our three-day elopement of a wedding, we poured another fraction of the cost of an average American ceremony into a villa in southern Italy. This time we invited about a dozen friends to join us.

We all chipped in. The place had an olive grove, a pizza grotto, a stocked wine cellar, fresh food deliveries, and a pool that seemed possessed of a curious ability to make the sun revolve around it and not the other way around.

We sat by that warm blue rectangle with bottles of wine and novels and bathing suits that seemed to get a little smaller by the day. Then our friends dispersed, and I moved alone into a hotel in Rome for a night. Tony, meanwhile, flew to Tel Aviv to pick up his kids for their summer in New York by way of Italy.

Kids were once again our number one topic of conversation.

We were trying.

"Try" was the operative word.

Our biggest problem was timing.

If we wanted to procreate, we needed to do it well ahead of the 2020 campaign or I felt like I'd be screwed professionally. Tony felt like there is never a good time to have kids, because no one ever has an eighteen-year window where work is light and their social schedule is clear. But some stretches are better than others.

About a month before our trip, we stood in the kitchen working out the dates. Tony's kids had just been with us for a school break, so we had half-dry markers handy. Tony tore off a rectangle of paper towel for notes.

He wrote on the towel: November 2020.

I told him that the primary debates for 2020 would start getting serious in the fall of 2019 and I calculated that if I wanted to use the full four-month maternity leave plus one month vacation offered by NBC (thank you very much), I'd need to have the baby by late spring 2019. That way I'd take maternity leave through the summer and I'd be able to return in the fall and not really miss a thing, politically speaking.

Tony wrote all this down: late spring 2019 (having baby), early summer (maternity leave).

We did some counting on our fingers. Then I told him I wanted to drink lots of wine in Italy on our honeymoon. So we did some more counting and recounting on our fingers.

Then the panic set in.

If we weren't pregnant by September of 2018 we'd have to wait until after the election. I'd be thirty-seven by then. Tony would be forty. Doable, but risky, especially with Tony's constant warning that kids will wear you out more than all the nightlife in the world ever could.

So we tried and tried. And we tried. And we tried some more. Until trying became the least sexy concept in the world. We worried not because a doctor told us we would struggle to conceive. But because until you try, you just don't know how easy or hard it's going to be for yourself. It's as if you have some really important equipment sitting out in the garage and one day—after decades of using it, but not really using it—you decide to see if it still actually works. It's truly miraculous when it does.

I was pregnant that fall.

CHAPTER THIRTEEN

"Katy Tur, Go Home!"

I was at a familiar place waiting on an unfamiliar sight: the arrival of Air Force One to a Trump rally. It was my first event in two years, my first since the 2016 campaign. I came because I could feel something breaking in America. It was the fall of 2018, just before the midterm elections.

Journalism is supposed to gather for an otherwise sprawling country a common set of facts. What to do with those facts is the stuff of politics and debate. But this dynamic had broken down and I wanted to understand why. For me journalism had always been—in addition to its role as a watchdog of democracy—a great big adventure, this wonderful gift from my parents. But from the moment I knew I was pregnant, journalism became something even more vital, even more essential, and even more personal. Not just a safeguard for the future but a safeguard for my future. My children's future.

It worried me that the truth did not seem to matter, that facts were worthless, and lies were winning. We as a country couldn't agree on whether the sky was blue, the grass was green, or water was wet.

Even worse, I worried that journalists might be making it worse, including me. I wanted to understand why and I wanted to see if there was a way to adjust. So I did what we do. I went out into the world to talk to people.

———

The Middle Georgia Regional Airport is about eleven miles out of Macon, just past Smiley's Flea Market, before the Kohl's distribution center. It has one big runway and very little parking, which meant the Trump faithful had to line up at an auxiliary site and get brought in by bus. This would chafe some people, but Trump rally-goers are not some people.

They arrived as though wrist-banded into a music festival. Trump-a-palooza. There were flags and buttons. Dozens of hats and novelty T-shirts. Most people were smiling and laughing, easy in the knowledge that everyone here thought like them. Others looked oddly determined, as if showing up for a pre-mission briefing. It was a little like a Facebook fan page come to life. Except for the first time in too long I had a chance to do more than just read the comments.

"Excuse me, sir!"

"Hello, ma'am!"

"Hey there, how are you?"

My crew and I set ourselves up on the tarmac, trying to flag people down.

The bleachers were maybe a hundred feet away inside a hangar, surrounding the president's podium. Behind the podium was a giant American flag and above that was a—and forgive me, this is just the brand name—Big Ass Fan. We had at least an hour before the president arrived, so everyone was free to wander and gander and that's what we did.

"Katy Tur! Katy Tur!"

A lot of the Trump supporters knew me. Or thought they knew me. They said my name in a kind of faux-baritone, part farm sound, part song lyric. Every time I'd turn and engage, hoping to flag the person down for a chat. But a lot of Trump supporters would refuse to speak with me. They accused me in advance of deceptive editing, of twisting the facts, of trying to embarrass them or the president.

"Fake news!"

"Katy Tur, go home!"

But the conversations eventually started to flow. I found that it didn't matter to people whether the president had improved their lives. They supported his fight unconditionally. One man, for example, had been in the grips of unemployment for years but told me the president was doing great work on the economy. An older woman said her number one issue was health care, and although Trump hadn't even come out with a plan in two years in office, she was confident he would soon and it would work out in the long run.

How much more time will you give him?

"Maybe six more months."

Will you vote for a Democrat if he fails?

She laughed.

"Never," she said. "I'll just be sad."

But at least these people were engaging with a reality we could both recognize.

Other people were not. They just were not. One man told me that dead people vote in every Georgia election, which is not true but when he said it he had the calm air of an oracle dispensing pure truth.

"I read articles," he explained.

"What sort of articles?" I asked.

"Articles and papers and stuff that have statistics and stuff."

Anything mainstream? He mentioned Facebook and Fox News, but his real media diet was "a lot of little side organizations that dig and find a lot of facts."

I ask him how he figured out who or what he was going to trust.

"Common sense," he said in a commonsense voice. "You know, pray about it. Think about it. If it sounds right, it is right."

It went on like this all afternoon.

In one of my last conversations, I talked to a man holding a skinny cigar. I decided to be as direct and personal as possible, not asking about abstract entities like "the mainstream media" but the particular journalist standing right in front of him. *Me.* Why didn't he believe *me*?

He was thrown for a moment, surprised, and then he started to think.

"Well," he said. "I don't really know you."

He accused me and the mainstream media of being more than 90 percent negative in what we report about President Trump.

"It's your job to tell the truth," he said.

"But if you think the truth is negative, that's not our fault," I said.

"If you're leaning 90 percent one way, how can it be the truth? It can't be."

And right about then I was reminded of something I'd learned on the campaign trail.

Our job is to elevate the facts that matter regardless of who they benefit. But to people like these Trump supporters, we're out to hurt Trump and help the Democrats. Because of that perception the president gets a free pass from his fans. He could in theory (or fact) screw up 90 percent of the time and they wouldn't blame him.

They'd blame *us*. They'd say *we* were shading reality, not reflecting it. Then they'd loathe us even more. And the cycle would continue. In that way, the worse the president performed, the more we'd be hated by covering it, and the more he'd be forgiven his failures.

I don't know how to break this pattern, because it's not just Republicans or Trump supporters who get a little confused on this point. The first time I got stopped on the street for my Trump coverage was during the campaign. Tony and I were walking in the West Village and a bike went past us, then skidded to a stop. The young man did an awkward tippy-toes reverse and said, "Katy Tur! I just want to say I love what you do. You're doing a great job."

"Thank you," I said.

And I meant it.

But later I thought, what was he talking about exactly? What about the job was "great" from his perspective? When I took my first book on tour, I realized that a lot of people—some of my viewers and my readers among them—didn't see me as a journalist. They saw me as a teammate.

"Why don't you always call him a liar?" one person asked, disappointed.

"Why don't you do more to get him out of office?" another asked, hopeful.

It got to the point where I'd cut off the question before it was finished.

"That's not my job," I would say. "I'm not on your team. I'm on the side of the facts. That's all."

But the comments continued. On the street. On social media. Some people would be outraged if I had a Republican on and asked constructive questions. They were also outraged if I had a Democrat on and asked anything other than softballs. It wasn't about getting to some sort of shared set of facts or sorting the best ideas for policy. It was about beating the other team. Plain and simple.

The day after that Trump rally, I anchored my show on the road, set up in front of a fountain in the center of Marietta, Georgia. We covered the midterms, which were high-stakes and important. But at 2:55 we were back from commercial and I read a little essay about the news itself.

"Public service announcement," I said. "We are not your safe space. We are a news organization. We bring you the news."

I ended with a line told to me by an old-school journalist during the campaign. It resonated and I agreed with it. Wholeheartedly. I wanted the public to hear it too.

"The news should make you uncomfortable," I said. "If everything you read or watch gives you comfort, you're doing it wrong."

It wasn't a perfect essay, but I expected some social media comments, perhaps even some cheers.

There was almost no reaction.

CHAPTER FOURTEEN

"Fake News Anchor"

Robert Mueller was finished.

It was a Friday in March, the last of the winter, the first rays of spring, and I was in my office when the news broke. I was tired, exhausted, nine months pregnant, well within the zone of full-term delivery, which was probably why it took me a few beats to figure out what to do with the news. I saw that Attorney General William Barr had written a letter to Congress, acknowledging that he was in possession of the "confidential report," and then I saw what I felt was a predicament in the form of a sentence: Barr said he may be able to release the "principal conclusions" as soon as "this weekend."

This. Fucking. Weekend.

The predicament was how do I convince MSNBC president Phil Griffin to let me anchor that weekend. But in retrospect, predicament is not the right word. Barr's letter was more like an enticement, a temptation.

So much has happened since the days of "Mueller Time" that it can be hard to remember the Mueller investigation was the biggest story of the Trump years, up to that moment. Special prosecutor Robert Mueller—former Marine, former FBI director, man who looks like he eats glass—had been appointed to look into whether the Trump campaign had conspired with Russia to win the 2016 election and whether Donald Trump or an ally had obstructed the search for justice in that investigation.

The probe had been happening in secret with virtually no leaks, and nothing but a series of indictments for the public to pore over. That had encouraged a lot of analysis, which veered into speculation, which careened into wishful thinking from political enemies of the president. They could all be wrong. Or, then again, they could all be right.

I wanted to be on television to cover it either way. I'd been reporting on Donald Trump every day and for most of my waking hours since before he was president. I was also about to disappear for five months on maternity leave. And I don't care what year it is, or where you work, or what your status is, if you're a woman disappearing for five months to be a mom, you will have some worries about how it affects your career. Are the worries helpful? No. But they're real.

I got the news in the seated position, which was a semipermanent position for me in those days. I couldn't even pick up a pen if it fell off my desk, not since last week when I tried and popped a button on my pants, then tried again and tore the seam on my shirt.

What I'm trying to say is, I was a big round pregnant lady now. And I was sitting down. And that was a disadvantage. Because in the hallway, I could hear people on the move: running, papers flailing, voices rising. Some of them were rushing to help with the breaking news in that very hour. But others were thinking the same thing I was thinking.

They knew that along executive row—right then, that very minute—a decision was being made. Actually, several decisions. First: we'd be in special coverage mode all weekend. That's a given. Second: the weekend anchoring lineup might change. But who would it change to? That's what was pending. The rush was on to figure it out.

So I rose. Or I tried to rise. I rocked first and then engaged my legs, which lifted my butt and pointed my stomach toward the upper-left-hand corner of the room. My arms were holding up my torso, quivering a little, preparing to thrust me into the upright position.

Annnnnnnd, we're perpendicular, people. This was good. This was very good.

I came around the desk, rotating my belly to brush past my wardrobe, and start striding for the door. I had almost reached it when I realized I was not wearing any shoes. Or socks. I considered my options. I've known Phil for years. He's seen me cry. He's never seen me barefoot in his office. Was this the time to start? No.

I retreated to the side of the desk, where my flats were, looking extra flat these days. In my pre-pregnant life, I could put these on in five seconds or less. It was just a matter of stepping into them. But now, my every step was a stomp and my feet were swollen. I was going to need to engage my hands.

I tried to plant my arm on the desk for support and bend at the hip but it was like trying to bend in half while holding an exercise ball. The toe method came next. I lined up the first shoe and then pinched the back of it with my big toe. At the same time, I reached down a hand and grabbed the flat. I repeated the procedure and collapsed into one of my visitor chairs, exhausted, head lolled back.

The seconds were ticking by. I started to imagine the anchoring slots disappearing, names filling blanks, careers going in new directions. But instead of getting more motivated, I got less motivated. I started to wonder whether I really wanted this at all. I had a nursery to prepare. A husband to enjoy. A life of nonparenthood to indulge for a few more precious weekends. Did I really want to give up a Saturday and a Sunday to the Mueller report?

I did.

I put on the flats and pushed off toward the elevator. My belly was a giant round face with a protruding nose previously known as my navel. I had a stretch shirt over this mass of new life, but it was not hiding much. I felt like a VW Beetle with a cape over it.

Phil was one floor up. Every elevator ride in 30 Rock is NBC's smallest studio tour. I can't ride a 30 Rock elevator without thinking of Fallon skits. Or news promos. The premise is always you never know who you'll meet. I remember one for Brian Williams's old show *Rock Center* where Brian is standing in the elevator and each new ding welcomes in another anchor or correspondent. Ted Koppel. Harry Smith. Kate Snow. Finally, Seth Meyers appears, the old host of "Weekend Update" on *SNL*.

"Fake news anchor," says Brian under his breath to Natalie Morales. "Not one of ours."

Phil was standing in his office, watching a bank of televisions. I said hello to his assistant, who probably expected me to pause and make a request, but I just kept moving, rolling by her like a boulder. Once I was in the room he couldn't help but look up.

"Hey Phil," I said. "I want to volunteer to anchor this weekend."

"You want to volunteer," he said.

"I want to volunteer," I said.

We both smirk a little.

He knows me well enough to realize this isn't a charitable offering. I'm not volunteering to anchor this weekend. I'm asking to anchor this weekend. I'm demanding it. I'm trying to write my own name into the lineup. And I'm up here in person because I want him to see from the look on my face that I am serious about this one. I know the story. I'm comfortable in the chair now after two years. I can handle anything that breaks.

He seemed to take this in.

"Okay," he said.

"Okay, yes?" I said.

"Okay, yes," he said looking at Yvette Miley, the news manager in charge of the weekends. "Just let us figure out the time."

"Not the mornings," I said.

"You sure you aren't going to give birth on air?" Yvette said, joking.

"It would be great for ratings," I joked back.

Back in my office, I texted Tony. Phil had scheduled me in the afternoon, 3 to 5 p.m. on both days.

I'd made a huge mistake.

———

Saturday was a big nothing.

Sunday felt like the same.

I launched into the hour with what we knew so far.

But we knew nothing more than we knew on Friday.

Under the rules of the special prosecutor, Mueller's work was done the moment he handed the finished report to the Justice Department. There was no additional obligation to release it publicly. Given the intense public interest, however, Attorney General William Barr said he hoped to offer at least the big takeaways—as he saw them—as soon as that weekend.

It doesn't sound like much of a news day but considering how little was known about the findings of the Mueller investigation (basically nothing), and considering how big the potential stakes of the investigation were (basically everything up to and including criminal charges for a sitting president), we were going big with the news.

Looking back, I wonder if we were set up from the beginning or if it just unfolded that way. I wonder if Barr got the Mueller report on Friday, huddled with his team, and realized that under the law he had total control over what happened next. I wonder if the entire rollout was choreographed for maximum political benefit.

Sunday afternoon, not Saturday, the better to drive coverage into the evening and Monday morning. A thirty-minute warning, the better to drive up viewership for what's to come. A Friday evening tease, the better to pull in dupes like me who decided to give up their weekend in order to sit in a little boat in the dark and wait for something to jump out of the water.

The next thirty minutes were a whole lot of dancing in place. We didn't know the substance of what was coming, so we showed a slow-motion carousel of Barr pictures, standard practice in the news industry. Each shot seemed to have a different emotion, a different scene. Barr outside. Barr walking. Barr testifying. Barr on a porch. Barr on a couch. Barr happy. Barr stern. Barr in a vest. Barr in a suit. The visual effect was automated and there was no intended editorial meaning in the photos.

But the human mind does the rest on its own. It says, we can see him! There he is! He's smiling! He's sad! He's on the move! Our brain's default setting is emotion not reason, feeling not fact. We are emotionally invested in the news, in politics. We can't help it. We're human.

At 3:35 p.m. that Sunday, I'm told by a producer that we expect to get a copy of the Mueller report, no, a copy of the summary, no, a copy of "it"—whatever "it" is, we still don't know—in two minutes via paper handout.

Why a paper handout? There was no time to follow that thought. It turned out to be a four-page letter from Barr, which we literally read out loud on live television. This kind of thing happened when a major Supreme Court decision came down, but that's different. That's a branch of government delivering a judgment.

This letter from Barr was a statement from a partisan defender of the president, a political appointee commenting on an investigation into the man who appointed him. It needed fact-checking and context like any other partisan statement, but we couldn't provide any of it because we did not know what the statement was based on. We hadn't seen the underlying report.

It was nuts.

Sometimes, looking back, I imagine an alternate version of that Sunday, a version where every news organization got the statement from Barr but none of us released it until we had more information. It was and still is an impossible fantasy. Even if we wanted to sit on it, to go through it first, to wait for the full report before we reported on the summary, to take the time to add the context it needed, we couldn't.

Well we could but it wouldn't make the situation better. Either the competition would do it and we'd be in a losing situation in terms of viewership which is an ugly truth of for-profit media companies. Or an outlet with the interests of the president in mind would do it and then accuse us, the "mainstream media," of silencing the Justice Department.

They're not reading it because it's good for President Trump, they'd yell. *See, they are biased. They're liars.* It was a no-win situation. Our entire coverage model is based off breaking news. We cover it live and as fast as we can. Waiting is rarely an option, rarely a real choice.

It's been that way for at least thirty years, since my parents shot one of, if not the first live police chase in America. Not since the red Cabriolet beat Matlock. A chase which, by the way, had no context itself and very little information. It was all action, just like Barr's summary.

Still, I wish the Barr letter had been put away until we had read the report itself. I wish I could go back in time, return to that Friday, make the pitch that we were all about to be used. About to cover a political statement about a report we have not seen, put out by a man we cannot take at face value, about a matter of the most urgent national importance.

A few weeks later, we'd learn that Mueller himself felt the letter was inadequate. That the investigation had identified "numerous links between the Russian government and the Trump campaign." That "the Russian government perceived it would benefit from a Trump presidency and worked to secure that outcome." That the campaign "expected it would benefit electorally from information stolen and released through Russian efforts." That although the investigation did not find a criminal case of conspiracy, it also couldn't be certain there was not one—in the face of lies, lost messages, uncooperative witnesses, and a president who submitted written answers rather than sit for an interview.

But by then I was at home with our new baby.

"We've Got to Get Him Out Now"

I woke up in a hospital room, my eyes still closed, my brain running through its usual checklist of being alive and getting all sorts of unusual, disorienting, confusing, and downright alarming answers. I did not know where I was. I did not know how I got there. I did not know why I felt so much pain. And then in the middle of all that a baby started crying. I opened my eyes and remembered it was my baby. My Teddy. My tiny son wrapped in what I would have assumed was a kitchen towel until that moment.

Theodore Bear Dokoupil was born on April 13, 2019, at 5:55 a.m., weighing just 6 pounds 4.5 ounces. I'm glad someone decided to write that down because my brain felt fogged, socked in like the California coastline in June. On my finger was some sort of device that measured my pulse and my oxygen levels. But the most finely calibrated machine in the room seemed to be my nerves. I felt sawed in two, or nearly sawed in two, and if you really want to know the truth of it, I did not feel like Teddy had been "born" at all. I didn't birth him. I didn't even feel it. He was sliced out of me. Taken by a scalpel and a set of hands. Removed.

I was supposed to heave and scream and push. I was supposed to sweat and swear and yell at my husband for doing this to me. I was supposed to hate every moment of it and to love it all at the same time. I was supposed to feel it. Wasn't I supposed to feel it? I wanted to feel it.

I had let my doctor induce me, on the belief that it would stave off this very outcome. "There's a lot of literature surrounding the benefits of being induced at thirty-nine weeks," she had told me. "The statistics show you're less likely to need a C-section."

Great, I thought. I was days away from my due date. Teddy felt huge inside me. I couldn't sleep. I couldn't breathe. I had a near-constant pain in my ribs. I couldn't keep going to work. I definitely did not want to be cut open. I certainly did not want to be stapled back shut.

I had told my bosses at MSNBC it was time to start my maternity leave. I told them the first week of April would be my last in the anchor chair before the baby. I said, "I'm ready for single occupancy." I meant it.

On the day of the inducement, though, I wasn't so sure. Did I really want to have the baby right now? Was I really ready? Did Tony and I need one more night alone? And what about work? The Mueller report was supposed to be out "by mid-April, if not sooner," according to William Barr. I was in the anchor chair when Barr's summary came out. Didn't I want to be in the chair again when the actual report came out? Didn't I want to get a chance to cover the genuine document?

I'd been covering President Trump since before he was president. If this was the end of his presidency, didn't I want to be on when

it happened? And if this was not the end of his presidency, didn't I want to be on then too?

Tony and I debated it on a walk to breakfast and we didn't come to any conclusion until I started to feel a little sick. I didn't want another cold without cold medicine (one of the many parts of pregnancy no one tells you about). That made the decision for me.

My doctor started me off on a drug to trigger my contractions. She paired that with a less modern tool of obstetrics: a long stick to break my water. I always thought the water break is supposed to be nature's big signal that something is about to happen. We've all seen it a hundred times in movies. The girl's water breaks, she gasps, there's a minor commotion as everyone heads toward the hospital. The screen fades to black—only to come up on a slightly red-cheeked new mother holding her quiet baby.

Yeah, no. That wasn't my experience. The doctor reached in like she was trying to light the pilot in the back of an old stove. I felt like a farm animal. I felt like it took her whole arm. I remember hating Tony for turning away and then a hot gush of liquid, not in a grocery store or a coffee shop or some other picturesque setting but in a cold, sterile hospital bed.

The next thing I felt was a screaming pain in my belly like someone had grabbed me from the inside and twisted, hard, then pulled downward. My first contraction. The epidural came next, thank you very much, then nothing for a long time. Then sleep, then more contractions, and more sleep. I didn't realize sleep was even an option during labor, but I didn't sleep long. I spiked a fever, started shivering. I remember loud beeping and a dozen white coats at my bedside.

"The baby's heart rate is dropping," one of them said. "We've got to get him out now," said another. "Tony will meet you in the OR. It will be fine. In two minutes you'll be a mom! We have to go."

My bed was wheeled down hallways, crashed through swinging doors, and the whole time I was crying. Sobbing. It was like an episode of *ER*, except I wasn't watching TV. I was the one lying in the stretcher. And I was scared. Scared I was going to lose the baby. Scared of being cut open. Scared I had made a selfish mistake. I thought I should have waited. I thought I should have let the baby come when the baby was ready, not when I was ready.

I was terrified but at the same time I was ashamed of being terrified. I was ashamed I wasn't braver. Ashamed of my tears. I kept apologizing to the nurses and to the anesthesiologist who was pumping up my epidural.

He kept asking me, "Can you feel this? How about now?"

I said, "yes" and "yes" and "yes" and finally "no."

Then I cried some more.

I thought I was pathetic and that they saw me that way too. I imagined them rolling their eyes at me. Annoyed they had to deal with someone so weak.

"Call Dad," I yelled, thinking my mother was still in the room. Dad was always my go-to in a crisis, my in-house paramedic for blisters and bumps on the head. In this terrifying moment, with all my defenses down, the little girl in me, I guess, still wanted my dad's official reassurance and confident declaration that "everything is going to be just fine." I wanted my dad to take care of me like when I was a child. But my dad wasn't there, was not going to be there. Was my mom with me? I couldn't be sure. I also couldn't be sure I was actually awake and speaking.

I felt like I was lying there for an eternity but Tony tells me it all happened in a matter of minutes. The tarp came up. The scalpel cut through my flesh. Teddy was out.

I remember listening for the scream that would tell me everything was all right. That Teddy was alive, that I didn't fuck it all up.

196

And thank goodness it came almost instantly. A moment later he was in my arms. Sort of. I was still flat on my back—on the other side of the tarp, my doctor was stapling up my lower half. It was the weirdest split screen in history: half gory surgery tent, half joyful hello.

It got even worse.

Teddy was placed on my chest. Just for a second. Long enough to take a picture. Then he was gone. Curtain closed. Game over. Visiting hours suspended. They didn't let me see him again for hours. They told me it was because I had an infection in my placenta and they weren't sure if he gave it to me or if I gave it to him. But they were absolutely sure that they needed to do some tests before it was safe for me to be with him. That made me cry again. And again. For my baby. For my own mom. I was hopped up on painkillers, exhausted, hungry, overwhelmed, and overwhelmingly sad.

They told me Teddy was in the continuing care nursery. They told me not to worry, but I worried. I wanted to see him. Would they at least roll me to the window? Show me he's okay? Sure, they said. When we bring you to your room. But then they didn't show me. They didn't roll me by the window. That made me cry even more.

Some hours later, Tony brought me a video of Teddy. He was holding him, stroking his tiny head, careful not to bother the wires that were stuck all over his impossibly small body. My mother was there too, holding the camera.

"He's a little furnace," Tony said to her.

"Talk to Katy," she said and Tony's happy face turned down a little. "She's going to feel bad."

I did. My son's first nights were in the care of strangers, in a loud, bright room, his family too far away to hear him if he cried. In the middle of all this, the nurses handed me a pump, showed me how to use it and told me to save whatever I could produce which was basically nothing.

They said, "Don't throw it out! That little drop of clear stuff is liquid gold. We'll put it in his bottle."

I felt like a failure. I felt like my body had let me down and I was somehow incapable of the thing I was made to do. And now my son was paying the price.

I can't remember when but at some point—hours and hours later—the tests came back and showed whatever they needed to show. Teddy was allowed to stay in the room with us, in a little plastic basin next to my bed.

I woke up and looked over at Tony, who was laid out on a little cot in the corner. His feet were still on the floor. His shoes were on. His clothes were on. His body was flat out, mouth open, surrounded by all our takeout food bags.

He woke up and handed Teddy to me with a kiss and a whisper. He said, "good job." He said, "he's beautiful." Then my first conscious moment as a mother: a feeding that I struggled to stay awake through. I drifted off and then woke up with a start, worried that I'd dropped the baby. This happened over and over for what felt like forever. When he was finally full, I immediately went back to sleep.

———

Sometime later a tall, skinny, German man was standing over my bed. He was talking to me but I had no idea what he was saying. He didn't leave but a new visitor appeared, my mother-in-law. She was somehow under the bed, knocking on a hidden door in the bottom of the mattress. She was getting angry that I wouldn't let her in. But I didn't know how to work that door and the German man wasn't helping me.

The next thing I knew the psych team was in the room. Who

exactly had I seen? What had they said? When did it happen? Was I awake or asleep? Was it a dream? Was I hallucinating? Was I eating? Could I concentrate? Was I happy? Did I want to hurt myself? Did I want to hurt the baby?

They were holding clipboards and looking at me with serious faces. I was smiling at them, trying to laugh it off. We all seemed to agree that what I'd described was a crazy story. The issue appeared to be our differing definitions of crazy. I meant it in the way that a dream is crazy. They meant it in the way that a new mother is potentially clinically psychotic.

How do you convince a person that you're sane?

Eventually the doctors left me alone.

They said, "Don't be afraid to tell someone if you start to feel differently."

They said, "Help is available."

They left their cards.

My first full day of motherhood passed like this and the next three passed as though they were happening to someone else. The hallucinations stopped. My catheter was removed. My incision was dressed and redressed. I used the bathroom on my own. I stood on my own. I sat and held Teddy on my own. I nursed him on my own. Then more visitors arrived. Real ones. Tony's older kids, my stepchildren, Teddy's brother and sister. They kissed Teddy on the head. Our mothers cried at the sight of him.

Every day Tony tried to get me to pose for a picture, something we could send to CBS and NBC, something for Instagram and Twitter and for those little announcements on television. The more he asked, though, the less I wanted to do it. I did not care if anyone cared and I knew Tony wasn't inherently thrilled about the idea.

He didn't love that I would constantly scroll Twitter, tweeting and retweeting, posting and reposting. I considered it to be an extension of my work. Tony considered it to be a distraction and a kind of con. "You're already paid to work for a media company," he said. "Why are you volunteering to work for a second media company?"

But things change. Tony was about to be announced as a co-anchor of *CBS Mornings*, the network's national morning show. It was a huge job. And nothing says morning television like a cute baby photo. So we eventually posed for the picture. Teddy in my arms. Tony leaning on the hospital bed. Us smiling at one another like the stork brought cookies and cash along with our bundle of joy. Tony's mom took the shot, then I used my phone to add enough filters and fades to make our photo look normal, aka like the other new mom shots we've all seen, aka not at all like new moms actually look.

The last item on our checklist before we could leave the hospital was a short video about shaking your baby. The main idea was that there is never a good time to shake your baby. Sound advice, no doubt, but also a very odd thing to say to someone. When you get a new car, they don't tell you not to crash it. When you get a new shirt, they don't tell you not to tear it. But when you have a baby, the state of New York offers a tutorial on not shaking your baby to death. The message is mandatory. It must be heard.

Tony and I laughed at first, then went silent, and then weepy as we watched the news-style interviews with grieving parents. I found it all unimaginable and extremely frightening. I remember thinking, what fresh hell is this going to be if they're reminding parents not to lose their tempers? Is that what happens to parents? They become murderous versions of themselves?

Tony and I sat for a moment after the video. Teddy was in his car seat on the floor, wearing a newborn onesie and a pair of newborn socks. He was so small the socks looked like they were going to fall off. The shirt puddled on his tiny chest. I was sitting on the side of the bed when Tony got up to look out the window. We could see part of the East River and Tony—now a father of three—was taking a deeply dad-like interest in the passing tugboats.

I must have had some sort of look on my face because while he stared at the boats, one of the nurses came and sat next to me. She'd been a regular visitor in our room since my first raving, wild-eyed night. She'd been there for the hours without Teddy and the first hours with him. She'd witnessed it all, including Tony's big boasts that he would remember from his previous tours how to give the baby a bottle, and how to change his diaper, and how to swaddle him to sleep. But you know what? He did. Now the nurse was sitting down to tell me it's true.

"I see a lot of husbands and most are useless," she said. "He's not. Just follow his lead."

I couldn't tell her the truth: that what I was worried about wasn't only baby care.

It was me. My identity. My career. Before Teddy was born, my biggest fear wasn't actually the pain of labor or the pushing or the tearing or even, God forbid, the emergency C-section that I actually ended up having. My biggest fear was the change. Or potential change. I was a journalist. I didn't know who I was if not a journalist. I was afraid I'd lose my edge and with it my job and my life. I was afraid my priorities would shift and I wouldn't be able to tell my bosses because this isn't the kind of job where that's possible. I was also afraid that my priorities wouldn't shift and I'd hate myself for it.

I said none of this. Instead, I gave her a hug and I whispered, "Thank you."

When she left I took a long look around the room and noticed how empty it had become. The grandmas were gone. The older kids were gone. And my father, well, my father wasn't there.

CHAPTER SIXTEEN

"Can I See Your Nipples?"

"It's KAMALLLAAAAAAAAAAAAAAA."

Right after we arrived home from the hospital, my phone rang. I was in the bathroom trying to get a moment alone, sitting on the toilet lid, breathing deeply and working up the courage to look down at the mesh hospital briefs I had just pulled around my knees. I knew it was going to be ugly. I wasn't sure I wanted to know how ugly.

I didn't even know my phone was in my hand until it started to flash and buzz, and I don't know why I looked at it except for the distraction. I was looking for any reason on earth not to look down. So even though it was a 415 number, San Francisco area code, a city where I know nobody, I picked up.

"Hello?" I said.

"Katy??"

The voice on the other side of the call sounded excited for me, like I was about to be presented with checks every week for the rest of my life.

"Yes?" I said.

The voice was iconic even then, midway through the 2020 campaign for president. It was the voice of Democratic candidate for the White House and senator from my home state of California, the voice of the current vice president of the United States, the voice of Kamala Harris.

But was it really her? Or was I still hallucinating? It took me a second to register what might be happening. I was groggy, half-drugged, self-pitying and the voice sang out the name like the announcer on a daytime talk show. I imagined Oprah, arms stretched out, head tilted back.

Is this a joke? This has to be a joke. Someone is pranking me.

"Hi???" I said.

"I heard you had the baby!!!!! I just wanted to call to say congratulations!"

Her voice was alive. It jumped out of the phone and danced around me like a technicolor rainbow.

OMG it's really her.

"Oh yeah," I said, still unable to do more than match the energy of a sulking twelve-year-old. "I did."

"How's the baby? How are YOU?"

I looked down.

Inside the briefs was a mat of gauze folded up like an origami diaper. A catchall for what was still falling out of my uterus. You think that when you push a baby out, you push everything out. Or you think, if you had a C-section, like I did, they just mop it up before they sew you up—not so different from a dentist after they remove a tooth.

But no.

Your body spent ten months building a home for another life and it takes weeks for that home to dislodge in pieces and flood down a swollen Mississippi of bodily fluid.

Six weeks, at least!

They do tell you this at a doctor's visit or you read about it in some book with a contented goddess on the cover. But nothing quite readies you for what actually comes out. They say it's like a really heavy period. That's being cute about it. What comes out is not cute. There will be blood. There will be tissue. There will be clots. Golf ball sized are normal. Baseball sized are not.

I thought about telling Vice President Harris the truth, making a joke of it all, telling her what I happened to be in the middle of doing, and maybe that would have been the right move.

But my professional filter kicked in. It suddenly occurred to me that this was a work call. I'd be covering this person, one way or another, once I got back to work. So I decided, maybe I don't tell her about the Carrie movie in my pants. Maybe I keep it upbeat. Build a bridge. Make a connection. Be human. The kind of human she'll agree to sit down to an interview with during the campaign or if it gets to that point, the White House. Be nice but be a reporter.

"I'm good!!!" I said, trying to find a spare barrel of excitement. "Teddy is good. We just got back home."

I felt like Harris had opened a door by calling me, but instead of walking through it, I banged my head against the frame. I was so flat, so lifeless. I was Morse code to her technicolor rainbow. She must have noticed it too because she begged off the call pretty quickly.

"Okay!" she said. "Well, I just wanted to say congratulations and good luck! Talk soon."

I immediately realized that I had failed a test my mother would have passed. She would have realized that while you might be taking some time off from the news business, the news business is never taking some time off from you. I was also failing on a frontier my father would have somehow conquered.

My father had always been looking for the next thing in news, never stopping, defying rules and regulations, risking life and limb. I wasn't going to be taking Teddy up in a helicopter anytime soon, but perhaps I should have been shooting video for social media? Above the neck anyway. Anything to keep this new me connected to the me that existed out in the world as a journalist.

But I was out of ideas. And out of energy.

I simply hung up and then sat there for a while longer forcing myself to look down.

———

"Would it be insane for me to come back to work for a day? Just for my show? Just for two p.m.?"

A few hours after the Kamala Harris call, I typed those words to my boss.

I did it in secret, because I knew Tony would remind me of my strongly held prior intention to forget about work and lean into motherhood. It was not that I had renounced that opinion. It was just that it felt like a historic moment for the country, the biggest story of my entire tenure in the anchor chair, except I wasn't in the anchor chair.

I was home. In the living room, my mom was watching TV with the volume on 109. Tony's mom was grinding more coffee in the kitchen—which is basically in the living room—which is basically in my bedroom.

The rental listing for this dream apartment of ours had described it as a two-bedroom with "sliding glass walls allowing for the open airy feel of true loft living." In fact, the glass walls were likely a legal requirement because the second bedroom had no windows. Either way, all that open airiness meant absolutely zero noise cancellation. This had been fine when it was just the two of us. Now there were two of us, plus a newborn, plus two older half-siblings, plus two very lovely, helpful grandmothers.

No matter the volume, no matter the location, I could hear everything from every corner of the home—usually in echo—thanks to the "12-foot-high ceilings throughout combined with white-washed brick walls" for that "refined yet contemporary ambiance."

My mom didn't even notice the noise. She was consumed by the image of an empty podium with the Department of Justice seal on the front. Underneath it was a giant red we-mean-business BREAKING NEWS banner and these words:

SOON: ATTY. GENERAL BRIEFS ON MUELLER REPORT.

This was the evidence behind the conclusions I had reported on . . . could it have just been a few weeks ago? It felt like a lifetime. I wanted to stay and watch the press conference. Then I wanted to go back into work. But this was a big day for another reason. It was Teddy's first full day back from the hospital and the day of his first pediatrician appointment, which is of course its own kind of history, personal history, the stuff that happens in a flash, they tell you, the stuff you don't get back, the stuff you're supposed to savor and treasure and turn into memory books and albums of baby's first year.

"KATY!!!!"

I had been lingering in the living room, planning my escape while Tony went downstairs with the baby.

"Baby, c'mon. We're going to be late!"

"I'm coming. I'm coming!"

I waddled down the stairs holding my belly. No one tells you this, but the waddle stays after the birth. And the belly. In my case, there was also the giant cut. None of which made it easy to live on the third floor of a New York City walk-up. I hustled as best as I could hustle. The sooner we got to the doctor, I figured, the sooner this would be over.

In the car, with the baby in the car seat between us, I started to lay more of the groundwork for my return to the anchor desk.

"Do you think they'll let me come in?" I said.

"The pediatrician? Of course they're going to let you come in."

"No. No. Work. Should I call Phil?"

"What? No. You had a baby five days ago. You're on leave. No."

Tony shook his head and broke eye contact, staring out the window in a way that communicated: I can't even look at this ridiculousness.

"You're right," I said.

That morning I'd woken up in my own bed for the first time as a mother. I'm not even sure it's accurate to say I woke up. That suggests a night of sleep. Had I sent a note to the chairman of NBC News at 3 a.m. describing my son as the evil dead spirit in *Game of Thrones* that is trying to destroy the world? I checked my phone. Yes, I did. (He did not reply.)

We arrived at the pediatrician, who was on the ground floor of an old brownstone in Park Slope, Brooklyn. It was the same doctor who had been seeing Tony's older kids since they were babies, a towering figure in the Brooklyn mommy world. We didn't even need to give the hospital an address or a phone number.

"Oh we know her," the nurse had said.

But when we walked in, I wondered if there hadn't been some sort of mix-up.

"Is this the right place?"

Tony nodded. I tried to readjust my expectations to include an old ripped couch, dust balls, and chipped paint. We checked in and

I checked my phone. I dragged my email down, looking for updates on Mueller. Nothing. I opened Twitter and did the same. Nothing. I opened text messages. Nothing.

Maybe everyone was just watching and waiting, I thought. Then I tried to text my mom and it didn't go through. This wasn't a lull in the coverage. This was a dead zone for cell service.

I wanted to scream.

I wanted to climb on the desk and shake the nurses until they gave up the office WiFi password. But I couldn't do that. That would be unseemly. Un-motherly. Un-well. I couldn't act un-well at my five-day-old's wellness checkup. What would the pediatrician think? What would the other mothers think?

The pediatrician called us back into an even smaller room with even less cell service. As we walked deeper into the office, I stared at my phone, trying to will it into some sort of connection with a cell tower.

"Hello!" the pediatrician said. "Welcome! And congratulations! How is little Theodore?"

"He's good," I said.

"Is he eating?"

"Yes," I said.

"Are you nursing?"

"Yes," I said.

My plan was to get through this as quickly as possible.

"Any issues with milk production?"

"No," I said.

Next we needed to weigh the baby. The doctor put a pee pad down on the scale, the kind you buy at the pet store for your dog. Then I laid Teddy down on it and he stretched out his bony legs and arms, grimaced and squeezed his eyes shut.

The doctor tapped the weight at the top of the scale to the left—

which counts ounces along with pounds—but the scale didn't move. She tapped it left again, and again, and again.

Teddy was a featherweight baby, no question about it. His diaper was smaller than my palm yet it looked huge on him, like a body pillow wrapped around a pencil.

"You really need to make sure he eats," the doctor said, suddenly more serious. "If he falls asleep, just wiggle your nipple in his mouth."

I nodded.

"We really appreciate your time," I said in the universal pose of a person leaving another person's office. The doctor seemed to misread the posture.

"I know how stressful this can be," she said. "I'm not rushed at all."

Shit!

More questions: "How many wet diapers does he have a day?"

I looked at Tony. I didn't even know we were supposed to be counting.

"Six," he said without a pause.

"What about poops?"

I looked at Tony again.

"Five."

I leaned forward again to leave, but Teddy started to cry. The doctor looked at him and I looked at him and I so badly wanted out of this dungeon but I knew what was expected of me. I knew that a "good" mother would not want to leave and go back to work. I had a light baby. I needed to feed him. The doctor needed to see me feed him.

"He's hungry," I said. "Do you mind if I take a couple minutes to nurse in here?"

The doctor smiled. She doesn't mind at all. In fact, she'd like to watch.

I used to be a person who changed quickly at the gym. Then I had a baby and another lady watched me breastfeed and I didn't even think twice about it.

"Can I see your nipples?" she said. "You have great nipples."

She meant for breastfeeding.

Teddy ate and then fell asleep and I took the opening.

"Thank you, Doctor."

I thought I caught some side-eye from Tony, but I ignored it and made for the door and beyond. The second we walked out my phone buzzed and chimed. There was more incoming than I could possibly keep up with. A lot of it was from my mother.

"They're pre-butting Mueller again!" she wrote. "This is insane!"

And that's when I did it. I opened up a new message and turned away from Tony.

"Hi, Phil," I began, texting my boss, putting my plan into motion. "Would it be insane for me to come back to work for a day? Just for my show? Just for two p.m.?"

When I looked up Tony was staring at me.

"What are you doing?" he asked.

"I texted Phil," I said.

"What?" he said. "You're insane."

"I can go in," I said. "It's just one day. My mom can hang out with Teddy in my office. It's just an hour for my show."

"Katy, you're bleeding. You have staples in your stomach. You haven't slept. You're on serious pain medication."

"It's fine," I said. "I can contain all of that for an hour."

My phone buzzed before Tony could respond. It was Phil.

"We love you," he said. "But that is crazy."

Tony read it too.

"See," he said. "Let's go for a walk."

We decided to walk all the way home. Teddy fell asleep. I didn't check my phone. The rest of New York City was at work, but we were wandering through its streets in the spring air. We had days and days with nothing to do but be a family. I began to feel the first pulls of it. That's why I didn't notice the stranger stopped in front of us.

A viewer.

"Oh, hello!" she said. "I was thinking about you today on television."

"Well, I actually gave birth a couple days ago," I said, nodding at the stroller. "So, you know."

She glanced at it, barely acknowledging the baby, then looked me dead in the eye.

"It must be killing you not to be at work right now."

———

For the next five months, I learned how to be a mother while also being a journalist. At first, I tried to keep up with a daily, sometimes hourly news cycle, while I was also breastfeeding, and pumping, and changing diapers, and soothing tears, and learning how not to accidentally kill my baby. It wasn't just hard. It felt impossible.

Story lines passed me by entirely. Others I couldn't bring myself to engage with. There was one about a father who was separated from his four-month-old. I don't know what happened next. I couldn't read through the story. The headline made me sob.

There had always been a certain amount of distance I could put between myself and the news. I could cover a plane crash, a shooting, a deadly wildfire or flood or hurricane, any of it, and be upset for the victims without being haunted by the tragedy. But after I became a mother, that separation was gone. It's like motherhood had given me an extra length of emotional nerve endings.

I reacted to details in a new more visceral way. The kid's book in the crash debris. The half-charred teddy bear. The waterlogged baby shoes. The images made my body seize up and my mind churn. Now, I don't just comprehend what happened; I experience an echo of it, a physical pain for the parents or the kids left behind.

But to my relief, I realized that I was also still me. I was a mother, yes, but I was also still a journalist and instead of one identity replacing the other, the two identities combined and seemed to double in size.

And yet.

I also worried.

I worried about my job, my profession, the public life of my country, the potential for violence amid all the lies, the rage in what used to be everyday politics, the limits of journalism to cover it or fix or stop any of it. I worried and all my worries braided in with my fears and the entire thing seemed to trail me everywhere.

That was me in the fall of 2019.

The happiest wife and mother in America, you might say, but also the grown-up version of that little girl who slept with a knife on the bedside table, her back to the wall.

CHAPTER SEVENTEEN

"It's Gonna Be Great"

A wind chime filled my head. I opened my eyes and quickly reached under my pillow. It was the alarm on my phone. On the other side of my room Teddy was sleeping in his crib, and I needed him to stay asleep for at least another hour, so I could get ready for work.

It was my first day back. I was ready. But a part of me was scared too. Every minute I had been gone had taken my mind further away from the anchor chair. Not covering the major stories, not being in daily contact with my sources, not being in the mix had exacerbated my already acute worry that I was a professional fraud just waiting to be sniffed out.

From the outside, my world probably looked secure. I'd had my own show for two years, ratings were strong. Empirically things looked solid. But I couldn't shake the nagging feeling that it was all gonna change when I came back. That it had already changed. Now that they've seen me gone, I worried, did they realize they never really needed me in the first place?

———

I tiptoed to the kitchen. As long as I was quiet, five-month-old Teddy should stay asleep for another hour. And I needed him to stay asleep for another hour. Because I had exactly one hour and fifteen minutes to get out of the house and the babysitter wouldn't show up for another sixty minutes. If he woke up my whole schedule would be thrown off and I'd be failing the whole working mom challenge right out of the gate.

In the kitchen, I grabbed a pair of small plastic bottles with yellow caps and two giant plastic funnels. I grabbed them with the care of a jewel thief. Because if a single cap fell to the floor, my day would fall to pieces. Gear in hand, I tiptoed back through the bedroom and into my bathroom, where I placed the stuff in the sink and ever-so-quietly shut the door.

There I paused, eyes shut tight, ears wide open, listening for the sound of a ruined day. But the whimper didn't come. I might make this flight after all. I checked the clock.

6:03 a.m.

I had given myself seventeen minutes to pump out a morning bottle for my son. I looked down at my shirt which was mostly dry for a change. Usually I woke up covered in milk. But last night I wore the pumping bra to bed to save time when I woke up. The breast pump was a double-action number. So I screwed a funnel top onto the two bottles I brought into the bathroom and then ran a long plastic tube from each bottle to the motor. The tubes supplied the pressure, the funnels grabbed the milk, and the bottles did what bottles do.

Then I maneuvered the funnels into place and twisted the dial. Medela calls this contraption the Pump In Style. But nothing about the image that stared back at me in the mirror could be described as stylish. I had bags under my eyes, my hair was greasy, my stomach was lumpy and there were two plastic tubes coming out of my bra. When I dared to look down, I didn't see nipples but udders—giant, fat, and distressingly long. I felt like a science experiment.

Then there was the sound of the pump itself, a hypnotic heaving and wheezing. Over time, and many sleepless days and nights my brain—in its endless search for meaning—turned the sound into words. Now I heard not a dumb pump but a jumpy robotic nag. It was saying over and over again:

"We've gotta leave. We've gotta leave. We've gotta leave."

In fact, we did. It was 6:20 a.m. I had ten minutes to shower and wash my hair.

To make the stakes even higher than they already were, MSNBC sent me to Washington as part of special coverage. Some Democrats were pushing to open impeachment hearings, citing hush money payments, corrupt pardons, and violations of the Emoluments Clause, which prevented the president from accepting something of value from a foreign government. The network wanted to go big. Almost the entire lineup would be broadcasting from inside the Capitol complex.

No pressure.

The shower was so hot it burned my skin at first. But I liked it like that, starting my day by sweating out the stress. I needed it too. I kept telling myself not to worry.

"It's gonna be great. A big splashy return. And you have a big splashy essay to end the show with."

I washed my hair, rinsed, and repeated. And I did the same with my little affirmation.

"It's gonna be great. A big splashy return. And you have a big splashy essay to end the show with."

Part of me had thought that being on maternity would be a little like being on vacation.

But no.

It turned out having a baby is nothing at all like a vacation. And that being a parent is just as much work, if not more, than actual work. I could feel the parents of the world screaming I TOLD YOU SO at me. I guess I just didn't believe it. I was a campaign reporter! I lived out of a suitcase for 510 days! I routinely woke up at five and went to bed at midnight! I turned off my personal cell phone because I couldn't answer texts! I ate peanut butter packets for dinner! What could be more consuming and exhausting than that?

A baby!

Nothing, not the long work hours, not the travel, not the peanut butter for dinner, not the lack of sleep, was harder or more demanding or more exhausting than parenting. And here was the proof: what I would give for a night alone in a hotel room. The irony.

Wait, what time is it?

I reached for my phone and the baby monitor.

Teddy, asleep.

Time, 6:40.

How was I in there for twenty minutes? I wondered. I had only shaved one of my legs. I decided to cheat on the other, quickly cleaning up the skin below the knee and ignoring everything above. My skirt was long enough.

I toweled off and recalibrated my plan. Instead of a full blow dry, I'd do a modified blow dry, quick and rough, and hope the D.C. hair and makeup team could help me out. I whipped my hair back and forth. Except I did it with the ginger force of a thirty-seven-year-old who was just cut in half and is prone to vertigo. Then I reached for the blow dryer and stopped short.

The hair dryer was a bad idea. Too loud. Too risky. I looked back at the baby monitor. Teddy was still knocked out cold. So I tiptoed out of the bathroom, out of my room, and into the living room, where I had laid out my clothes the night before.

"Wahhhhh."

Clock check. 7 a.m., on the dot.

"Mama's coming bubba!"

He was on his back looking up at me with big bright eyes. He came out so small but now he was a bruiser. I mean that seriously. With the short blond stubble on his head, he looked like a baby boxer. He looked up at me, probably thinking that today was going to be like every other day. That we'd get up together, snuggle skin to skin, eat a little breakfast, watch Daddy on morning television, and then go for a walk. But today . . . would he realize I'm not there? Would he know if I didn't come back?

I could feel the panic rising inside me. My heart started beating faster and the room started getting hot. Thankfully the moment was broken by a knock on the door. Julia, our babysitter, was here. I picked Teddy up and let her in.

"Good morning, Mom!" said Julia. "Ready for the big day?"

"I think so. You guys going to be okay?"

"Yes, of course we will! And we'll make sure to watch Mama at two! But they should have let you work from New York."

Julia was full of well-meaning "they shoulds" about my bosses.

"Can't change it now," I said. "There's fresh milk in the refrigerator. The bottles in the front are from last night. Behind that is this morning's milk. I'm defrosting another bag from the freezer. If you need more, boil a bowl of water in the microwave and then put the milk bottle in the bowl. Don't microwave the milk itself. And use the oldest bag you can find in the freezer. Something from May."

Julia knew all this. But I couldn't stop myself from repeating it just in case. Julia let me talk and nodded along.

I handed her Teddy and rushed to get the rest of my things. Back on the campaign trail I had my daily checklist memorized. Now I can't remember which boob I last nursed with. So I wrote it all down on a piece of paper that I left on the counter.

Backpack, check.

Computer, check.

Makeup, check.

Notepad, check.

Change of clothes, check.

Cooler bag, check.

Ice packs, check.

Empty bottles, check.

Pump . . .

Oh shit.

I ran to get the pump and the used boob funnels from the bathroom. I was tempted to just throw it all in a bag and go but if I didn't clean them they'd start smelling of rotten milk. I checked the clock, 7:12. The car was downstairs, and if I wanted spare time to deal with a potential argument at TSA over my freezer bag and ice packs, I had to be on the road by 7:15.

So I poured dish soap on the funnels—put them in a bowl—and turned on the hot water. They could soak for a hot second while I finished piling all of my loose ends into a canvas bag. It was an oversized tote I got from the Sydney Writers' Festival the year before. As in Sydney, Australia. A place I was able to jump on a plane and fly to without thinking too hard about the TSA. I don't know if I subconsciously intended it by picking this bag on this day but it was a reminder that I'd done big things and had earned my position.

It should not have been so easy to forget. But I often did. Instead of swaggering around, laureled and feeling well-liked, I sometimes felt small, lacking, unworthy of my anchor chair. And it wasn't just me. Other women in the business have shared similar self-doubts. Maybe they develop in any competitive industry, eating away at the confidence of men and women alike. Or maybe in addition to the glass ceiling women—especially moms—face a sinking foundation, a baseline of success or seniority that's just a little less solid than a man's. In any case, I tried to remind myself of everything I had done in my more than fifteen years in journalism. Local news. Breaking news. National and international news. Packages and live shots. Big sit-down interviews. Quick man-on-the-street conversations. The craziest campaign in modern American history. And years now in an anchor chair.

"It's gonna be great," I told myself again. "A big splashy return. And you have a big splashy essay to end the show with."

No time to rinse. I shook off the cones and dropped them in the bag.

"Bubba, Mama's leaving!" I said as I bent over to give Teddy one last goodbye kiss. He was on his playmat, absorbed by the colors and shapes.

"I love you. I'll see you when you wake up tomorrow. Be nice to Julia."

And then I ran. If I stayed a second longer I wouldn't leave.

———

"One more thing, today is my return from maternity leave, which is either my first day back to work or my first day off from the other job I've been doing for the last five months—caring for my newborn."

That's how I began an essay to close out my first show back. I told viewers just about everything about Teddy's birth and my time off. The C-section, the fact that my cut had gotten infected, the fact that Teddy was born healthy—but small, really small: 6 pounds 4.5

ounces, small. I told them that a few days later he got even smaller, down to 5 pounds 15 ounces—smaller than 93 percent of babies in America.

It was fine, so long as he gained it back, which meant he needed to eat and eat and eat and eat. Which wasn't easy, not only because of the C-section but because breast milk isn't the instant grab-n-go ready-made meal you might think before you suddenly try to produce it.

I told them about how scared I was to leave the hospital, and about how helpful it was to have Tony around—changing diapers, bringing me food, letting me nap. I was telling them all to make a point.

"Nothing about this story is exceptional—except for the fact that I got more time to figure it out than the majority of new moms in this country. And Tony got more time than at least 70 percent of fathers out there. And that is insane. It is insane that 25 percent of women go back after two weeks. And I think it's insane that seven out of ten men go back after ten days or less."

I was on a roll so I kept going, filling more than three minutes of airtime with an essay that was still coming to me as I was saying it. Sometimes what gets said on television would be inelegant or seem simple if printed in a newspaper. But sometimes that's exactly what makes television so powerful.

"Parents. Need. Time. With. Their. Babies," I said. "Babies. Need. Time. With. Their. Parents. And Moms need support. And if that support is coming from a partner, that partner should get equal time off. Paid time off. Emphasis on paid. Family leave supports babies, which supports us all."

Then I added a bit more because I was sitting there in front of the Capitol.

"The people who work around here, who work in that building

behind me, on this hill, talk about figuring out paid family leave. But for some reason it hasn't gotten done. Hasn't even gotten a vote. And that is shameful."

The word "shameful" came out with a little more relish on it than I might have intended. But I was feeling that way in the moment.

Years later, with still no law on paid leave, it is a depressing reminder that even when everyone agrees, even when the well-being of families, and parents, and babies is at stake, Washington still doesn't work.

CHAPTER EIGHTEEN

"Happy New Year!"

The most beautiful place on earth is section 109, row 7, at Madison Square Garden on December 31, 2019, with ten seconds to go before midnight. One arm was around my husband. The other was waving in the air, cutting through the clouds of what we'll officially record as patchouli. Above my head were giant nets holding thousands of multicolored balloons. In front of me, down six rows and maybe fifty feet away, were dozens of dancers, dressed in yellow, red, green, and blue.

They were supposed to be clones of the four guys suspended in air above them who were jamming out to a song that had no lyrics and to the uninitiated, no melody either. It was a little hard to explain how they got to this moment, but suffice to say that about ten minutes before, the guys in the air were on the stage, gathered around a single microphone singing an a cappella version of "Send in the Clowns."

But they replaced the word clowns with the word clones. And when they were done, these clones flooded the stage and started dancing to the music. Although dancing was a generous description. It's more like they were forming and dissolving a series of patterns. It kind of looked like they're playing a big game of human Tetris. But then again that could have been the patchouli talking.

This was Phish's annual New Year's Eve show and this was their year-ender bit. It was trippy and I was all in. I listened to Phish in college, then stopped until I started covering Donald Trump. Now I'd found that it was the only thing that could steady my nerves and slow my brain. And after an impeachment in 2019, and all the Russia drama of the past three years I was ready for a change of subject. We all were.

I looked around at the twenty thousand people dancing and hugging and smiling and thought what a wonderful world this was. How amazing humans are.

We're all the same.

We're all doing our best.

We just want to be happy.

And I was happy. In that moment I felt weightless. Optimistic. Sure that everything, everywhere would work out just fine.

I looked at my husband and smiled as we both yelled out 3, 2, 1, Happy New Year!

The nets released the balloons and we were lost in a riot of color like pieces of confetti in a rainbow snow globe. We brushed away a pink one, then a yellow one, and then we kissed.

"I love you."

"I love you too."

"Twenty twenty is going to be a great—" POP.

Our happy declarations were drowned out by a spray of pops.

A guy in the row in front of me was stomping on the balloons—

bursting a literal bubble, shattering a snow globe of goodwill and optimism and fellow feeling.

It felt like an omen and suddenly 2020 came at me harder. I thought of the primaries, the debates, the general election. I imagined a return of the name-calling and the ugly rallies, the violence, the division. It was all going to come to a head. Just like 2016 all over again. Except now everyone knew the stakes. Except this time would be worse.

I shook my head like an Etch A Sketch, trying to clear it, and for a few minutes it worked. The patchouli kicked in again. The band was on an elevated platform, jamming in this baby of a year. But then I noticed that the platform was actually four individual platforms, one for each member of the band. Jon Fishman, Page McConnell, and Mike Gordon all came down in a fluid, synchronized descent. But Trey Anastasio, the lead singer, was still up there. His platform was stuck, and this was a terrible, no good, very bad omen for 2020.

CHAPTER NINETEEN.

"Are We Going to Keep Our Jobs?"

By mid-April, New York City had been on lockdown for more than a month. Outside hospitals were overrun with patients, and bodies. Not far from our building in Brooklyn, bodies were being stacked in the back of refrigerated eighteen-wheelers. Funeral homes had bodies piled like firewood in rooms once used for receptions. The city was lowering the poor and unclaimed into pine caskets and dropping those into the clay in Potter's Field. And every day it got worse, the sirens carrying for miles over an otherwise silent city. Each day I would wipe down the groceries. The counter. The floors. What if we had inadvertently stepped on something outside? What if Teddy had touched something?

Every surface felt like a death trap. The health professionals kept telling us: Wash your hands, scrub your wrists, and make sure not to miss your fingernails. Twenty seconds is the minimum. Sing "Happy Birthday" to time it out. Buy hand sanitizer. Stay inside. Be socially distant. Slow the spread. Like everyone else, I was paralyzed with fear and anxiety.

People who were able to leave the city had made a run for it. But we were still here, broadcasting from our basement, no option to leave. We were in a city shut down by a pandemic wondering if we were going to lose everything. Outside, 750,000 people were applying for unemployment benefits each week.

I woke up not only alone but in silence. For the first time in my life as a New Yorker, I heard birds in the morning, and it scared the shit out of me.

Tony had already left for his show. But he didn't go far. CBS and NBC had closed their studios and instead commandeered our half-finished basement, squeezing two full camera setups into a space that couldn't fit a pool table. Tony broadcast in the morning from one side of the room. In the afternoon I went down and broadcast from the other.

By the time I opened my eyes at 7:15, Tony was already downstairs, almost done with his A block—TV speak for the opening section of a show, usually the harder, more serious stories. Right now, it was all coronavirus. Nearly three thousand people had died of the virus. A month ago, fewer than a hundred. A month before that none at all. From zero to thousands.

When MSNBC asked if they could set up that camera in my basement, I'd requested a timetable.

"When am I coming back to the studio?" I wondered.

"I don't know."

"Is everyone going home?"

"That's the goal."

"Are we going to keep our jobs?"

"I hope so."

I glanced at my phone to see if Tony was asking me for anything. During the first few weeks of our new lives, working from home, I was his production assistant, printing him scripts, getting him coffee, and being an all-around gofer. He would then do the same for me on my show at 2 p.m. Since no one else was allowed in the house, we had to help each other. It was like a fun screwball comedy, back and forth, up and down the stairs, a real team, just the two of us. We quickly realized we could do it all on our own. Turn on the robotic cameras, fire up the lights and the tablet, and you could do a respectable version of a national newscast from your basement.

Well, sort of.

A couple of months later Tony went back to the studio. An ensemble morning show didn't work when all its anchors were in separate locations and on delay.

But I stayed in my basement for more than a year. Just me, the camera, and the voices inside my head—both real and imagined.

It got dark down there in the white studio lights MSNBC had set up for me. I felt isolated and alone. I was sure that every time my phone rang it was going to be one of my bosses telling me they had to cut back and that I was out of a job. I thought maybe they'd have a reason. I did fuck up a tweet about Kim Jong-un. They were not happy about it.

The call never came but I still worried. And in my worry I started to wonder just like everyone did. What was I doing with my life? Was this job worth it? Was I happy? Without the daily commute, the gossip in the halls, the debates about coverage in our shared office during our morning meetings, the studio and the crew, the travel, the source meetings, and coffee runs, I felt lost.

The pandemic was scaring the shit of me but the country was even scarier. We weren't just debating politics anymore, or partisanship, or bullshit about crowd numbers, the country was arguing over science—with more and more Americans denying the most fundamental information we have. We were debating life and death and still not finding common ground. Looking into my camera some days I wondered if I was even on air. Then I wondered if it even mattered if I wasn't.

CHAPTER TWENTY

"Congratulations! Today Is Your Day"

I thought I was going to explode. I was five months pregnant and I had been in the anchor chair for four hours without a commercial break, which meant without a pee break either. It was January 6, 2021, and I'd been co-anchoring all afternoon with Chuck Todd and Andrea Mitchell, waiting for Congress to review electoral college returns.

Most years, this assignment involved senators opening envelopes, some fusty lines about everything being "regular in form and authentic," and all of us going home on time.

Not this year.

I was also out of my basement, back in the studio, on set in New York while Chuck and Andrea were in Washington, D.C. Chuck was passing the coverage to Brian Williams and Nicolle Wallace and although I could keep my bladder in check if they'd let me stay, the prospect of relief had me counting the seconds.

We were in rolling coverage, live and unedited with no definitive end time, because the Capitol—the U.S. Capitol, the one with the dome, secure since the War of 1812—had been overrun, occupied and ransacked by hundreds or even thousands of supporters of Donald J. Trump.

The day reminded me how much I truly value this job and how much I love breaking news. But this was a new level of breaking news. This was breaking news about our country breaking. It was overwhelming and depressing and infuriating and sad. All the lies, the misinformation and disinformation, the gaslighting, the partisanship, the anger, and the threats over the last five years came to an epic culmination.

There was a Trump-inspired mob inside the Capitol, hunting for lawmakers, fighting with police. The vice president was evacuated. The Capitol Police lost control. The U.S. constitutional process itself was delayed, if not denied, as men and women in Make America Great Again hats and carrying TRUMP 2020 flags fought to overturn the results of the election.

Part of what made me upset was the predictability of this moment. The warnings were obvious and they started months ago when President Trump said he couldn't lose the election unless it was rigged. Then when he lost, he said it was indeed rigged—ripped away by fraud. From election night all the way through to that afternoon, he kept repeating that lie of a stolen election.

He kept it up through lawsuits—which he lost, and where, by the way, his lawyers didn't argue fraud because you can't lie in court. He kept it up through pressure on elections officials, which is not fair game and we're lucky it failed. Maybe most importantly, he kept it up through an almost daily direct appeal to his supporters. And what do you know? They showed up for his fight.

Because one plus one equals two.

But I felt like I was somehow to blame. How did it get to this point? Why did the president's Big Lie survive? Wasn't it our job to correct it out of existence, to police the truth, and make sure the American people know the facts? Did we not do our job?

––––––

A voice in my ear: "You're clear, Katy."

I wanted to stay but, dear Lord, I needed to leave.

I unclipped my microphone and looked for someone, anyone to talk to. But the studio was a wasteland, empty along with most of the building—a casualty of the coronavirus pandemic. Gone was the buzz that follows a broadcast, the feeling like mission control after a successful launch. Gone were the smiles and the atta-boys and the jokes you tell each other to manage your worst fears. Gone were the greenrooms and the makeup rooms and the halls for nonstop conversation and did-that-really-happen debriefs. Gone was everything that usually made 30 Rock feel like home.

In its place was a Mars-like silence.

I could hear my shoes squeak as I pushed into the hallway, phone in hand, mind racing. It occurred to me—not for the first time—that walking around with a phone in your hand was like running with scissors: inherently dangerous, an accident waiting to happen, risky, ill-advised, the dumbest thing we all do every day. A phone is a weapon and with it you could end your career at any time. It wouldn't take much either. I could do it right now.

I pushed open the bathroom door and solved one of my problems. The other problem just kept getting worse. My mind replayed the assault on the Capitol, testing and retesting my assumptions about everything. I thought back to that Trump rally outside of Macon. I should have seen this violent break with reality coming. Should have seen that maybe none of the last five years of reporting really mattered. That maybe not enough people were listening. Not enough people trusted it. That maybe that's why the president was able to spin up a lie about a stolen election and millions upon millions of Americans were right there to believe him. Forget politics. Forget parties. Forget elections themselves. That is an astounding failure of one man's character but isn't it also an astounding failure of a country's free press?

I kept thinking. This lie about fraud didn't just go back to the election or even the lead-up to the election. This went back to 2016. Accepted wisdom at the time was that there was no way he could beat Hillary Clinton. Sources in his campaign even told me that Trump himself didn't believe he could beat her. That's why in the weeks before that November he started going on about a conspiracy to keep him from office.

"There's a global power structure," designed to rip off the working class with Clinton at the helm, he said on election night 2016, early on when it looked like he was losing. He was laying the groundwork to call it all rigged, if he needed to, even back then. Why were any of us surprised he would do it again in 2020 and that doing it again would summon a violent mob?

A man had told me—on camera—at a rally over the summer in Pennsylvania, just a few months ago, that he was willing to do "whatever it takes" if Trump lost the election. There was no way Trump could lose, he said, unless the whole thing was rigged. He was listening. Others were listening. They took Trump seriously *and* literally.

Walking back to my office, the afternoon was coming back to me in screeches and whirls. I felt like I was on the brink of doing something stupid. I was angry. I was frustrated. I was scared. Like all tragedies it had started as a farce. Andrea and Chuck and I came on at noon and we wished each other and the viewers a Happy New

Year. Hadn't 2020 just been an awful year? Sure had been. Hope we're on to better things.

We went to White House correspondent Kelly O'Donnell. She was covering the president's speech at a rally on Freedom Plaza, a short walk from the Capitol, less than an hour before Congress was scheduled to convene. The banner behind President Trump said "SAVE AMERICA." Other banners said, "STOP THE STEAL." He was behind bulletproof glass, delivering essentially the final rally speech of his presidency—his last stand—before the big eviction on January 20. He'd been pumping up the event for weeks on Twitter.

December 19: "Statistically impossible to have lost the 2020 Election. Big protest in D.C. on January 6th. Be there, will be wild!"

December 26: "Never give up. See everyone in DC on January 6th."

January 1 (a retweet): "The calvary [sic] is coming Mr President! January 6th."

Kelly described the anger of the speech itself, much of it directed at fellow Republicans, much of it directed at Mike Pence, and said: "Probably the most dominant word that has been used today has been fight."

Amazingly, at the moment she said this, we could also hear the president. He was saying, "We're going to walk down to the Capitol," and we could see in a split screen that some of the crowd had already come to the Capitol. We tossed to another correspondent, Ellison Barber, who had already made the connection between the speech and the crowd now encircling the building.

"A lot of people here were playing the video of that speech," she said, "listening to it, reacting to it in real time."

She pointed to one part of the crowd in particular, a group

near some sort of a road or an access point. A black motorcade had just driven by and the assumption was that Mike Pence was in that car, looking out at the crowd, hearing the chants in his direction: "FIGHT FOR TRUMP, FIGHT FOR TRUMP."

"This is not a fight they are going to give up on easily," Ellison said in closing.

So there it was. All right before us. In front of us. For weeks. And then hours. And then minutes. The president's rhetoric, his speech, his supporters, their anger—all of it directed at the Capitol. We had the inputs. We had the equation of the day, the one plus one equals two. Why couldn't we stop it?

I turned on the television and saw our same mix of camera shots. It brought my mind back to the cameras inside the building, dipping into the joint session of Congress before it had been disrupted. It began with shuffling papers, the senators milling around, Vice President Pence looking confused. Nancy Pelosi looking uncertain too. Four years had passed since anyone had done this and it seemed no one could remember how it went.

At one point, the papers were sorted but the mics weren't working. It was actually kind of charming. Here were our elected officials, in the greatest deliberative body in the world, gathering to mete out judgment on weighty matters of national importance, while also wondering "is this thing on?"

Maybe that's what had lulled us a little. The common humanity of it all. The thought that for all the rhetoric from the president, and all the rhetoric from his allies in Congress, our elected officials would do the right thing in the end. Because they're us. *We the people.* But the next thing I remember is the standing ovation, a cheer in support of objecting to the vote count, of not certifying the election, of trying to somehow give Donald Trump a win he did not earn.

The states were to be counted alphabetically, which meant Alabama first—a win for President Trump. Mike Pence had the gavel. He asked the assembled members: "Are there any objections to counting the certificate of votes from the state of Alabama that the teller has verified appears to be regular in form and authentic?"

There were none.

Next up, Alaska, another win for President Trump, another routine review. Any objections?

There were none.

It was when the same question was asked of Arizona, the first state Trump had lost, Representative Paul Gosar rose to speak. Outside, Trump supporters were in a standoff with police, trying to shove their way into the building. The pictures were all over social media.

He said of the count, "I object," and he cited sixty of his colleagues.

Pence said, "Is the objection in writing and signed by a senator?"

We knew there were always going to be House Republicans willing to make the objection no matter what—people like Matt Gaetz and Mo Brooks whose entire political livelihood was tied to showboating for President Trump. In past years, Democrats in the House had done the same. But there was no way a Republican senator would sign on to this, right? The senators were supposed to be our catchers in the rye, protecting the country from running off a cliff.

Senator Ted Cruz rose to speak.

"Yes it is," he said, a hand in his pocket.

Someone shouted no. Others booed. But the reaction that lingered was the applause, a slow build from a few claps to a sustained standing ovation by all or nearly all the Republicans.

That's when something amazing happened.

The full Congress divided into separate sessions of the Senate and House to debate the Arizona objection. In the Senate, Majority Leader Mitch McConnell rose to speak. For the last four years he had supported the president because the president supported his agenda. He also of course became majority leader while his wife took a cabinet position.

But here he was condemning his colleagues for their objections to the count, warning of "a death spiral for democracy." He blamed the president and unnamed others—"powerful people"—for lying about the election results. It was moving stuff, a speech that sounded like history as soon as you heard it.

But you could argue Mitch McConnell was one of those powerful people. He didn't lie about the election results, but he didn't push back on a whole host of other lies from President Trump over the past four years. Maybe, you could argue, he was *privately* uncomfortable with the president's attacks on our allies, or on immigrants, or on free trade, or on science. Maybe, you could argue, he recoiled from the president's decision to wink at white supremacists and play down the coronavirus. But he and his party rarely did more than occasionally shake their heads. They might admit to feeling "troubled" or "concerned" by the president's behavior. But most of the time, he was still their guy. To this day, for most of them, he is still their guy.

McConnell's speech was not enough to save the day.

In the middle of his words, in fact, a producer sent me a social media video of the protesters outside. It was a film we were not yet seeing in the studio, where we were still in a state of default normality, reassuring ourselves and our viewers that while there was an angry mob outside—the Capitol Police was surely prepared. And don't forget the Secret Service. And there's also the DC Metro Police. And wouldn't the National Guard be on standby?

At the very moment that Mitch McConnell was speaking, at the very moment he said, "I will not pretend this is a harmless protest vote," the video my producer sent me showed Donald Trump supporters in hand-to-hand combat with Capitol Police. The video showed that a protest gathering had tipped toward rioting and that cheers and chants had turned into kicks and punches. In other words, at the very moment the highest ranking Republican in Congress was standing up for truth at last, the lies were breaking through.

I was scared to talk about it on air. I did not want to say anything that hadn't been confirmed ten times over. Especially on a day like this, in a country that felt as though it were teetering on the brink of something very dangerous. I did not want to be the person who tipped it over. But what I was seeing was happening. I needed to trust my eyes.

"Look, this McConnell speech doesn't come in a vacuum," I began, recounting the ways the speaker had helped create the situation he was now denouncing. "But when he said 'I can't pretend that this is going to be a harmless protest vote,' at that very moment"—*I felt a flutter as I prepared to report an escalation that felt urgent and important but that we hadn't yet shown on TV*—"At that very moment, according to video circulating online, there were Trump supporters storming the steps of the Capitol, trying to get in, getting pepper-sprayed by Capitol Police."

Chuck moved on, tossing to former Missouri Democratic senator Claire McCaskill, who began yet another regular political analysis of McConnell's speech. It turned out to be a last coat of normalcy.

The videos on social media kept coming and kept getting worse.

The day, possibly the country, was going to pieces.

The normalcy finally broke when Oklahoma senator James Lankford paused while talking about the count in Arizona. We had no sound, but his eyes screamed confusion, then alarm. His jaw tightened. A man had run up to him, leaned in to say something. Then our shot switched to a wide angle of the Senate dais and that's when I noticed that the vice president was missing from the frame.

I squinted my eyes, leaned toward the biggest monitor in 30 Rock.

Chuck must have been doing the same thing because he and I cut in at almost the same time. Our congressional correspondent Garrett Haake was on it too.

"There's something happening . . ."

"I'm looking . . ."

"In the Senate . . ."

"On the right-hand side of your screen . . ."

"Let's go into the Senate . . ."

"What's going on . . ."

"Let's hear sound please . . ."

We quieted down and waited but there was no sound. Just the image of men in suits waving at people to get down.

The Senate had cut its camera mics.

"It seemed like," I said, my voice caught between a desperate need to get it out, and deep fear of getting it wrong. "It seemed like they just ushered Mike Pence out really quickly."

"They sure did," said Chuck. "That's exactly what just happened there."

Then the camera itself went dark.

———

In my office, I pulled out a pad to get some of this down. It was now well after 4 p.m. But the protesters still had control of the building. My phone buzzed. The president tweeted out a video of his own. He was directly addressing a camera on the White House lawn.

"I know your pain," he began.

Whose pain? The rioters?

"I know your pain," he continued.

The rioters.

"We had an election that was stolen from us."

Lie.

"It was a landslide election and everyone knows it."

He wouldn't back down. The claim was bogus but his supporters believed him more than they believed us. That was the reality of the moment.

A couple of hours earlier, after the siege had begun, the president tweeted something else. This was after the vice president had been evacuated, after both chambers of Congress had been shut down. But when I looked at the tweet, I thought for a moment it had to be fake.

I had covered the *Access Hollywood* tape, I had been the first person on television with it after *The Washington Post* broke the story, and I remember the sheer disbelief of quoting the then-Republican candidate for president grabbing women by the "p-word." I felt like I was getting played. That's part of what made Trump so hard to cover. He could be literally incredible. As in: not credible. As in: impossible to believe.

And yet.

"Mike Pence didn't have the courage to do what should have been done to protect our Country and our Constitution, giving States a chance to certify a corrected set of facts, not the fraudulent or inaccurate ones which they were asked to previously certify. USA demands the truth!"

That was the tweet.

I started to say the president was "incorrect," but actually it was more than incorrect when he had every chance to provide evidence of fraud and he had not done so. It's more than incorrect when every state in America has certified the vote count. It's more than incorrect when his supporters are rampaging through the Capitol.

"It is *lies*," I said. "Remember, he told them to go do this."

———

I went home to read my son a story and put him to bed. I wanted to drown out the day. But on the drive home my mind drifted back to the worst moment of the afternoon.

It had happened around 3 p.m.

"What are we looking at here? Oh my gosh. Oh my gosh."

I cut in over Chuck and Andrea. I can't even remember who they were talking to.

"Guys, we gotta interrupt."

A woman's face filled the screen, her head turned to the side, toward our camera in a video we didn't know we would show and would not show again. Her eyes were open but unblinking. Vacant. She was gurgling blood. I remember thinking, she's not going to make it.

Just before I got home, I learned I was right.

The woman was dead.

I wanted to cry but I also didn't. I wanted to feel but I also didn't. Instead, I did what I've done so many times in my life, and especially the past five years. I balled up the entire disgusting day and put it into a little compartment for later. I have a warehouse or two somewhere in my brain full of these balls of trauma delayed, feelings denied. All the terrible sights and sounds and behaviors we'd all witnessed and somehow had to absorb for 1,800 days and counting. All the stuff I've had to take in and translate to a public, half of whom don't want to hear it, don't want to see it, hate me for mentioning it.

Then I walked inside.

My son, Teddy, was nearly two and pure joy. He was doing circles in the kitchen. Pushing his "big truck" around and around the dining table. I wanted to grab him and hug him tight. Bury my face in his messy head of blond curls and breathe in his innocence. But he wiggled free of my arms.

Upstairs, in bed, we read *Oh, The Places You'll Go!*

"Congratulations! Today is your day. You're off to Great Places! You're off and away!"

I thought of a list I made in my office, an accounting of where I might go and what I might do to get away from this job and this country. Could I drop out of this life, leave the reporting on this nightmare to others? Could I move back to London? Could I move to Paris? Is there some sort of Greek or Italian connection Tony or I can pull? Maybe, but no. I turned back to Teddy. Soon he'll be a big brother. We'll be a family of six including Tony's older kids.

We're not off to great places, not off and away.

We live *here*.

We have to make *here* work.

And I have to make *me* work.

Epilogue

In probably the most bizarre tape in my parents' library—stranger than even the guy who painted himself red, put on devil's horns, and went for a naked run on the side of the 10 freeway—my father put the camera on a tripod and aimed it at a brown leather couch in my parents' first apartment together, somewhere in Santa Monica. On the tape my mother is on the couch alone while my father makes adjustments. But she isn't totally alone.

She's surrounded by at least a dozen stuffed bears. Big ones. Small ones. A black bear. A polar bear. A bear in a bow tie. A bear in a scarf. She's in a blue tunic and white turtleneck with a press pass dangling from a lanyard around her neck. If you saw this person today, you'd think: hipster reporter for VICE.

My father appears and nestles himself in among the bears, putting some on his lap. He's wearing a brown plaid shirt and big aviator-style glasses with clear lenses. They have what looks like the same shaggy, feathered hairstyle. And they are in love. It's obvious. She's twenty-eight and he's twenty-three. They talk to each other

247

in soft little cartoon voices, until they turn to the camera and begin a goofy but earnest video letter to their unborn child.

To me.

"Hello, we're talking to you through the miracle of modern technology," my mother says. "You might want to know why we have this camera. Well, this is the camera your father does all the work with and how he"—she pauses—"how we both make money."

My father cuts in, weirdly serious for a guy on a couch surrounded by bears talking to a fetus.

"We have a sole business called Los Angeles News Service and we go to breaking news events."

My mother points to me in her "stomach" and adds that I've already been to all sorts of interesting places.

"Fires."

"Yeah."

"Rainstorms."

"Yeah, rainstorms."

"And you'll see yourself being born," my father adds.

"No, you won't."

"Yes, you will."

"No, you won't."

They're both smiling.

"We'll work this out," my father says.

My mom won. No such video exists.

Eventually, they spend a significant chunk of time introducing me to each bear, by name, one by one.

"Snowy . . . Cutest . . . Baby . . . Silly . . . Happiest . . . Honey . . . Littlest . . . Pooh . . . Dearest . . . Sweetheart . . . Darling . . . Sleepy . . . Flattest . . . and Tiniest . . ."

Then they sign off as though it's one of their live news reports.

"Here in Santa Monica, I'm Robert Tur."

"I'm Marika Gerrard Tur."

They kiss.

When my mother gets up to turn the camera off, my father's eyes never leave her. She adds one more message for me before the tape stops rolling.

"You're probably going to think we're nuts," she says.

Yes, Mom, I do.

I also think you're really sweet and the video makes me smile. It reminds me that you two really did love each other and you were excited about loving me and my brother.

Moments like this are what make the archive, and my childhood, so confusing. Sometimes the video adds up to a portrait of the most amazing, loving, and exceptional family, a kind of traveling circus of journalists, with kids and parents and Grandma Judy. Other times, the moments are ugly or scary or sad. Or all three.

I understand *why* it turned out this way.

I'll never understand why it *had* to.

So where are we now? It turns out that writing a memoir is a lot like driving at night, except not only in fog, as E. L. Doctorow once said of writing in general, but through freezing rain and ice. You can only see as far as your headlights and the road may not hold you. But slowly, slowly, ever so slowly, you can still find your way home. That's me right now. I can't tell you the future. I can't even promise we'll get there. But here's as far as the headlights show.

My father and I are texting again, if only barely. I send kid pictures and she offers perfunctory replies. We're not talking by phone, not hanging out in person. She hasn't met Tony or Teddy or Eloise, who arrived in the spring of 2021. Eloise's middle name is Judy Bear, by the way, a continuation of my parents' devotion to bears, and in honor of my late grandmother, my father's mother. Judy was the only person I know who might have been able to give that chapter of my life a happy ending.

But Eloise Judy Bear is still too young to talk, let alone channel the wisdom of her namesake. She can't tell me what to do next. Or whether this book was a good idea. She certainly can't talk my dad through it. I do wonder and worry what she, my dad, will think of it. I hope she appreciates that it's honest. On some level, I think she might have known it was coming and maybe even wanted it this way.

When I reread that old *New York Times* piece, which included quotes from my father, I was surprised to see her almost willing this project into existence, summoning it from her keyboard to my own.

"About my transition," she wrote to the reporter, "no child should have to deal with a father in transition from male to female. Perhaps it will be the subject of Katy's second book!"

Not exactly, Dad, but not far off.

Maybe this will open a door, start a new chapter. Maybe one of us will call, and one of us will pick up, and we'll start talking. Then again, maybe we won't, and it's possible that's for the best. After all, I'm dealing with the past already.

A couple of years ago, I threw a potato at my husband's head. I was pregnant and exhausted by a mess he'd made in the kitchen. He was annoyed because he'd cooked and I didn't seem to care. We bickered a little and then I exploded. No warning. Just rage. I saw the potato in flight before I realized I was the one who threw it. But I've decided that's on me, not my father. No one can choose the gifts of their childhood. But everyone can work to reject its worst lessons. That's what I'm trying to do.

My dad has said she worked as hard as she possibly could to rid herself of the rage she'd learned from her own father. I don't know how she's doing now, but she failed when we were kids and we still haven't had a real conversation about it. Not long ago, though, she did open up to a documentary filmmaker. She said all that rage had been a problem for her, but also a solution. It kept her alive as a child, helped her escape her abusive father and succeed as a journalist in the macho world of breaking news.

"Before the sex change and the estrogen, I was infused with this wonder drug called testosterone, and testosterone in my system really equals asshole," she says in one of the clips. "So I was uniquely built to challenge the other testosterone-driven assholes, in many cases those that wore badges."

The archive is full of these face-offs and they're spellbinding.

Dad tapping a cop in the chest with a microphone, daring him to call for backup. Dad agreeing to drop the camera to fight a security guard in an alley. "You're going to go to jail," says a big state trooper with a handlebar mustache, wagging a finger in my father's face. Dad doesn't back down. "You don't know what the fuck you're talking about," my dad says. "You ever heard of California code 405?" One altercation ends with the cop punching my father, hard. "Did you get that? Did you get him hitting me?" Dad says, almost giddy.

The results speak for themselves. In the film, she says rage made her "a very good newsperson," and for her time and place it's hard to disagree. If she was on a story, there was no stopping her. She always got the shot. But in that documentary she also admits to a darker side, describing her rage as "incompatible" with friendship and family life.

"If you live long enough, you'll hurt people, and if there's any good in you, you'll regret it," she said in an interview from a home I've never visited somewhere in the California mountains. "I regret, I regret, I regret every single day some of the despicable things I've done."

She didn't say it to me. But it's still good to hear it.

For all the turmoil, all the pain, I'm happy. I've grown to appreciate that life is never one thing at a time. It's always giving and taking, not in turn but all at once, and I have to admit that it's given me a lot. I found a partner. I started a family. Despite all the sitcom clichés about marriage and children, Tony and I are still crazy about one another.

We made two beautiful babies together, meaning I now have four curious, beautiful kids in my life to show me what tomorrow will be like. Considering that Tony and I have each written memoirs about our crazy upbringings, all the kids are hereby authorized—as far as we're concerned—to write about all the ways we'll inevitably let them down.

Just know we tried.

Remember that we were softies when it came to cookies and bedtime. Also, by necessity, cartoons. (One of you is watching a second animated movie of the day *right now* just so Mommy can finish her book.)

My life's other great gift is a bit like having children. It feels like a mixed blessing in some moments, but it's a treasure in retrospect. I'm talking about journalism.

Years ago, I did a lot of stories about lottery winners, including jackpots that ran into the hundreds of millions of dollars. My colleagues would inevitably start daydreaming about what they'd do if they won. Sometimes there'd even be a pot going around the office. If the numbers came in, you'd get a chunk of the money big enough to quit your journalism job forever. Back then I remember thinking, who would want to quit journalism?

I knew I was in trouble when I started thinking: me.

I'm past that now. Or at least I think I am.

I've come to realize that journalism really is the worst job on the planet like motherhood is the worst job on the planet. It's messy and often absurdly unpleasant and you're constantly judged by strangers and, yes, there must be many other wonderful ways to lead your life. But I've written a whole book at this point and I can't think of any.

I still worry about the future and about failing. I worry about my kids and my country. But I remind myself that I'm not in control. Journalism can't save us. Perfect parenting can't save us. Our lives are one long rough draft and none of us will know how we've done until many years from now, long after the memories have gone cold, and maybe not even then.

All we can do is try.

Acknowledgments

I said at the top, this book isn't supposed to exist. It does now because I realized it was a book I had to write, but also because a long list of good, generous people helped make it possible.

To Julia Cheiffetz and the team at One Signal, Atria, and Simon & Schuster, including Jonathan Karp, Libby McGuire, Joanna Pinsker, Dana Trocker, Wendy Sheanin, Nick Ciani, and Amara Balan, thank you for the patience and the patience and the still more patience as I slowly came around to what had to be done, and then even more slowly figured out how to do it. You gave me time and space and understanding. Most important, you wouldn't let me give up. A writer can't ask for more.

To Glynnis MacNicol, thank you for grabbing me by the shoulders, pointing me toward the darker corners of my past, and showing me that I was in fact brave enough to confront them, even if I did wriggle free and run a few times. Without you (and a sometimes immoderate amount of wine and tequila and lamb vindaloo) this book would have been glossy garbage.

To Matt Yoka, who spent years trying to figure out my family and still more years carefully crafting our story. *Whirlybird* is a triumph.

To Alan Berger and Rachel Adler, thank you for reading ten different false start versions of the first chapter and always telling me it was "great." I needed it every time.

To Andrea James, thank you for the conversations about what it means to transition, and how to write about it with care. Thank you also for being a perceptive reader.

To Mark Leibovich, thank you for picking up the phone when I needed help to see what was interesting and what was not.

To Aaron Volkman and Kerrie Wudyka and my entire MSNBC team, thank you for keeping the show together and, in key moments, keeping me together. Perhaps the next slow news day will actually be slow.

To Rashida Jones, thank you for putting me on TV once upon a time at the Weather Channel and still today. I promise I will never say the two-letter initials of a certain restaurant chain on air ever again.

To MSNBC, NBC News, WNBC, the Weather Channel, WPIX, News12 Brooklyn, HDNet, KTLA, and everyone I have been lucky enough to call a colleague, thank you for the journalism. There wouldn't be much point without an audience, but it wouldn't be possible without you.

To Jake Sherman, Bradd Jaffy, and Erika Masonhall, thank you for reading early versions and telling me—despite my doubts—that, yes, the story was good, and, no, I'm not a self-absorbed jerk for writing two memoirs before the age of forty. I promise there won't be a third. Not in this decade.

To Jonathan Lyons, thank you for reading the fine print.

To Julia Greenidge, thank you for helping us make it all work and for loving our kids as much as we do.

Acknowledgments

To Gail Felice: In your son Tony, you made a more perfect man for me than any Weird Science experiment I could've attempted. Thank you for Tony, and thank you for all the heart-to-hearts.

To my brother, Jamie Bear, I love you. We made it. Now you're a doctor. A Doc-Tur. I will never get tired of that joke.

To Connie and Gerry and Judy, I miss you every single day. I wish you could meet your great-grandkids.

To my husband, Tony, who lived this book with me as I relived its contents. I once told you there were no clean decisions, everything has its own complications. I was wrong. Marrying you was the cleanest and least complicated decision I have ever made. To borrow a promise from the gospel of Randy Travis, I'm going to love you forever, forever and ever, amen.

To my dad. I love you. I miss you. I wish things were better.

Finally, writing a memoir shouldn't be about settling old scores. But there is one score that needs to be adjusted. After the L.A. Riots, my parents' coverage of the Reginald Denny beating earned a Breaking News Emmy. If you look at the citation, though, you'll see my dad's name alongside a couple of KCOP staffers. What you won't see is my mother's name. She was the one who hung out of the helicopter to shoot that video. She was the one with the bullet hole in a camera battery below her seat. But the station needed space for the news director and the assignment editor, so the men in charge took the only woman involved off the list.

It wasn't the only time. Throughout my parents' career together, my mom didn't get the credit she deserved. She was quiet and shy while my dad was loud and showy. She was easier to ignore. But she was every bit as good a journalist. Brave. Smart. Cool under pressure. And without her, Los Angeles News Service would never have made it.

The truth is, I wouldn't have made it either. Thank you, Mom. I love you.

About the Author

Katy Tur is the anchor of *Katy Tur Reports* on MSNBC, a correspondent for NBC News, and the author of the *New York Times*
bestseller *Unbelievable*. Tur is the recipient of a 2017 Walter Cronkite
Award for Excellence in Television Political Journalism. She lives in
New York City.

ROUGH DRAFT

KATY TUR

This reading group guide for Rough Draft includes an introduction, discussion questions, and ideas for enhancing your book club. The suggested questions are intended to help your reading group find new and interesting angles and topics for your discussion. We hope that these ideas will enrich your conversation and increase your enjoyment of the book.

Introduction

When a box from her mother showed up on Katy Tur's doorstep, months into the pandemic and just as she learned she was pregnant with her second child, she didn't know what to expect. The box contained thousands of hours of video—the work of her pioneering helicopter-journalist parents. They grew rich and famous for their aerial coverage of Madonna and Sean Penn's secret wedding, the Reginald Denny beating in the 1992 Los Angeles riots, and O. J. Simpson's notorious run in the white Bronco. To Tur, these family videos were an inheritance of sorts, and a reminder of who she was before her own breakout success as a reporter.

In *Rough Draft*, Tur writes about her eccentric and volatile California childhood, punctuated by forest fires, earthquakes, and police chases—all seen from a thousand feet in the air. She recounts her complicated relationship with a father who was magnetic, ambitious, and, at times, frightening. And she charts her own survival from local reporter to globe-trotting foreign correspondent, running from her past. Tur also opens up for the first time about her struggles with burnout and impostor syndrome, her stumbles in the anchor chair, and her relationship with *CBS Mornings* anchor Tony Dokoupil (who quite possibly had an even crazier childhood than she did).

Intimate and captivating, *Rough Draft* explores the gift and curse of family legacy, examines the roles and responsibilities of the news, and asks the question: *To what extent do we each get to write our own story?*

Topics and Questions for Discussion

1. In 2020 Katy discusses feeling burnout in her career, due to the news, motherhood, and a global pandemic. Have you ever experienced burnout? How did you manage it and find ways to recover?

2. Both at the beginning of her career and even now, Katy often discusses the feeling of "impostor syndrome," despite her successes. Have you ever struggled with impostor syndrome—persistent self-doubts about one's abilities despite accomplishments—in your career or other parts of your life? How have you managed it?

3. In chapter 14, "Fake News Anchor," Katy is pregnant right before the release of the Mueller report and says, "I don't care what year it is, or where you work, or what your status is, if you're a woman disappearing for five months to be a mom, you will have some worries about how it affects your career. Are the worries helpful? No. But they're real." Have you had to balance motherhood and your career before? How did you feel it affected your experience in the

workplace and your thoughts about the role of work in your life?

4. After Katy's son Teddy is born, she worries, "I didn't know who I was if not a journalist." Do you feel that your job is a large part of your identity? Why, or why not? And how has your answer shifted over the course of your life?

5. In the chapter titled "Can I See Your Nipples?", Katy describes herself as "the happiest wife and mother in America, you might say, but also the grown-up version of that little girl who slept with a knife on the bedside table, her back to the wall." Are there elements of your family life or upbringing that you feel you have to hide? How do they affect your day-to-day life, relationships, or your reactions to stressful situations?

6. Throughout the book, Katy discusses her father's transition and how she processed the changes in their relationship. Have you had a parent or someone close to you transition? How did you feel navigating that experience? Did any of the feelings or reactions Katy describes resonate with you?

7. Katy describes her parents' work as the Los Angeles News Service and how it helped to pioneer the modern 24-hour news cycle, noting in chapter 2, "It felt like at any moment the world might split open for some poor soul and my parents would be thrown

into action." How do you feel about the relentless news coverage we now have access to through cable news and social media?

8. Los Angeles and New York are both characters within the book, backdrops to many of Katy's most defining moments. In chapter 2 she thinks of raising her children, noting "they'll never know Los Angeles as a native. In a sense, I worry that means they'll never really know me." Do you feel a significant connection to your hometown? If you have children, have you thought of how their childhoods might differ if they were raised somewhere else?

9. Leading up to 2017, Katy observes, "More people than ever were watching or reading the news. But fewer people than ever were trusting it." What do you think has contributed to this loss of trust? Do you trust the news and reporters that you watch or read? How has that trust changed in the last decade?

10. When Katy was not assigned as NBC's White House correspondent (in chapter 10, "Now the Fun Begins"), she writes, "I had Tony. Tony was in New York. Choosing life over career, for the first time, felt good. It felt right. My motto used to be, 'why be happy when you can be great.' Now it felt like why not try being both." Have you ever had to make a choice between your career and your family? What did it feel like at the time, and how do you think about it now?

11. In chapter 5, Katy comically breaks her front tooth just before an important job interview, and she has to talk her way into a last-minute dentist appointment. Do you have a crazy job interview story? How did you react, and what did you learn from it?

12. In chapter 5's job interview, Katy is told by the news director that her "boobs look[ed] too big in her TV clothes" and that she had to change her haircut to match one of the preselected photos he showed her. Have you ever experienced sexism in the workplace? How did you manage it or fight back? Have you ever felt the need or expectation to change your appearance for a job? How did that affect your self-image or feeling of self-respect?

13. In chapter 10, Katy tells the story of Tony's proposal to her in their living room in front of the "sad blue couch" and how it was a "simple honest proposal for a simple honest love." Do you have a special proposal story? How did the place and time tie in to your love story? Were you surprised? If you're not married but plan to be, do you know what kind of proposal you would envision?

14. In the moments before Katy says yes to Tony's proposal, she thinks about her loss of independence and the change to a life of partnership. Have you ever felt this way about a relationship? Did you feel you had to make compromises or change aspects of your life? How did that make you feel at the time, and now?

15. In chapter 18, Katy describes the bliss of Phish's New Year's Eve concert and how their music became the only thing that could steady her nerves in the wake of her reporting on Trump. Do you have bands or albums that have served as a source of comfort in your life? What would be *your* ideal version of Katy's Phish New Year's Eve concert?

Enhance Your Book Club

1. Read Tur's first memoir, *Unbelievable: My Front-Row Seat to the Craziest Campaign in American History*, and discuss it in contrast to *Rough Draft*.

2. For more information on Katy Tur and *Rough Draft*, follow her on Instagram and Twitter @KatyTurNBC.